Current Topics in Library and Information Practice

Repositories for Print

Strategies for Access, Preservation and Democracy

Edited by
Pentti Vattulainen and Steve O'Connor

DE GRUYTER
SAUR

ISBN 978-3-11-053324-8
e-ISBN (PDF) 978-3-11-053537-2
e-ISBN (EPUB) 978-3-11-053339-2
ISSN 2191-2742

Library of Congress Cataloging-in-Publication Data
A CIP catalog record for this book has been applied for at the Library of Congress.

Bibliographic information published by the Deutsche Nationalbibliothek
The Deutsche Nationalbibliothek lists this publication in the Deutsche Nationalbibliografie;
detailed bibliographic data are available on the Internet at http://dnb.dnb.de.

© 2018 Walter de Gruyter GmbH, Berlin/Boston
Typesetting: RoyalStandard, Hong Kong
Printing and binding: CPI books GmbH, Leck
♻ Printed on acid-free paper
Printed in Germany

www.degruyter.com

MIX
Papier aus verantwor-
tungsvollen Quellen
FSC® C083411

Table of contents

List of abbreviations

ABES	Bibliographic Agency of Higher Education, the
ACM	Association for Computing Machinery
ACS	American Chemical Society, the
ANDS	Australian National Data Service, the
APS	American Physical Society, the
ARL	Association of Research Libraries, the
ASERL	Association of South East Research Libraries, the
ASRS	Automated Storage and Retrieval System
BRGF	*Biblioteca Rector Gabriel Ferraté*
BUZH	Libraries of the University of Zurich
CARM	CAVAL Archive and Research Materals
CAVAL	Cooperative Action by Victorian Academic Libraries
CBUC	Consortium of Academic Libraries of Catalonia, the
CCUC	*Catalog Col·lectiu de les Universitats de Catalunya*
COLLEX	Collections of Excellence for Research
CONZUL	Council of New Zealand University Libraries
COPPUL	Consortium of Prairie and Pacific University Libraries, the
CRAI	Learning and Resource Centres
CRIS	Current Research Information Systems
CRL	Canadian Research Libraries
CSLS	Cooperative Storage Library Switzerland, the
CSUC	Consortium of Academic Services, Catalonia, the
CTLes	Centre Technique du Livre de L'enseignement Supérieur
DMP	Data Management Plan
EPICo	European Print Initiatives Collaboration, the
GATT	General Agreement on Tariffs and Trade
GEPA	*Garantia d'Espaiper a la Preservació de l'Accés*
HKSAR	Hong Kong Special Administrative Region
HKU	University of Hong Kong, the
HSS	Humanities and Social Science
HVAC	Heating, Ventilation and Air Conditioning
IDS	Information Network of the University Libraries of German Speaking Switzerland, the/*Informationsverbund Deutschsheiz*
IFLA	International Federation of Library Associations and Institutions, the
ILL	Interlibrary Loans
IOP	Institute of Physics, the
JULAC	Joint University Libraries Advisory Committee, the
JURA	Joint Universities Research Archive, the

JSTOR	Journal Storage
KEMO	*Austrian Academic Library Consortium, the/Kooperation E-Median Österreich*
LHL	Linda Hall Library of Science, Engineering and Technology, the
LIDDAS	Local Interlending and Document Delivery Administration System
LMS	Library Management System
LOCKSS	"Lots of Copies Keep Stuff Safe" Project, the
LRS	Learning Resources Catalogue
NLN	National Library of Norway, the
NPV	Net Present Value costs
NRL	National Repository Library of Finland, the
OBSVG	Austrian Library Network, the/*Österreichische Bilbiothekenverbund und Service GmbH*
OCLC	Online Computer Library Center, the
PCP	Periodical Conservation Plans
PRC	Peoples Republic of China, the
RDM	Research Data Management
ReCAP	Research Collections and Preservation Consortium, the
SCTR	School of Cultural Texts and Records, the
SLSP	Swiss Library Service Platform, the
SOAS	School of Oriental and African Studies, the
STEM	Sciences, Technology, Engineering and Mathematics
SUDOC	Système Universitaire de Documentation
U21	Universities 21
UB	University of Barcelona, the
UB BS	Library of the University of Basel
UB SG	Library of the University of St Gallen
ubifo	Council of Austrian Universities, the/*Forum de Universitätatsbiblio-theken Österreichs*
UGC	Universities Grants Commission, the
UKRR	United Kingdom Research Reserve, the
UNZ	Universities New Zealand/*Te Pokai Tara*
UPC	Polytechnic University of Catalonia, the/*Universitat Politècnica de Catalunya*
URV	*Universitat Rovira i Virgili*
WEST	Western Regional Storage Trust, the
WMS	Warehouse Management System
WTO	World Trade Organisation, the
ZHB LU	Central and University Library of Luzern
ZB SO	Central Library of Solothurn
ZB ZH	Central Library of Zurich

Steve O'Connor and Pentti Vattulainen
1 Introduction and Background

Every book should have at it's heart a simple idea. The simple idea links many of the arguments into an overview. Repositories have been collecting much of the world's published output for the purpose of supporting long-term access to published material, scholarship and the ideal of democracy. The simple notion for this book is that this ambition needs to be evaluated, re-scaled and perhaps re-purposed.

From simple aims for this book, complex papers are included in this volume of chapters by experts in this area. The chapters are drawn from experiences across the globe. They describe work to understand present and future collecting. They present work on developing new repositories individual and cooperative. There are descriptions of national systems and the review of their performance. Most of this volume is a statement of existing and evolving practice in an area which has been working powerfully but has been neglected. It has not been properly tested and found wanting but found difficult and left untried. Still, many have succeeded. These papers are a strong testament providing solid foundations for new models and directions.

Print Repositories are solitary places where the print materials rest easily in 'book musty-perfumed' comfort. Paper is the only medium with guaranteed archival permanence. But the value of repositories is, of course, deeper than this.

A Repository is, at its simplest level, an extension of a Library. It has been used as the off-site storage facility for lesser used materials. In this way, Repositories have been a part of the library and information infrastructure for many decades. Mostly they were established supporting individual institutions. This expanded in the 1960's with the establishment of cooperative repositories. This was due to the dual forces of economic constraint when funds were less available for each institution to have its own Repository but also because of the rapidly increased rate of publication and the inability to shelve all of this material in the on-campus library. The operating purpose and procedures of these cooperative repositories usually differed significantly as there was no 'standard' set of procedures to draw upon. Then again none of the education systems in which these repositories arose had the same strength or vision.

There, of course, are many differing models in different countries. These cooperative systems have largely worked earlier and better in countries with central government systems but not always. The United Kingdom had a very strong State Library in the British Library. It, in turn, had a large document delivery system in Boston Spa which discouraged regional libraries to do

https://doi.org/10.1515/9783110535372-001

anything else but rely on Boston Spa. The National Repository Library of Finland has always been impressive collecting material from all sectors of library across the country. The Australian system in CAVAL was established by the academic libraries in Victoria only but services Australia. The new system being established in France will be country-wide. So there is not a single model designed for all. There is no single solution.

The two simple ideas which libraries have largely embraced is that everything is available digitally. This is simply not true and will never be so. The second idea embraced by libraries is that they should now turn around, having purchased their entire print collections, and buy them again often as subscriptions without ever gaining ownership of that digital material. The new business model is fundamentally flawed in that access to published material is increasingly not available to the readers and researchers in our populations[1]. Content is only available through the large research and state libraries with the very significant resources available to them. The design of what is being collected is now a matter of considerable research and concern bibliographically and economically.

The shadow aspect to all of these deliberations is an element which affects the day-to-day workings of democracy. The impact of these fundamental changes will have a severe effect on our Democracies. A Democracy without information being freely available to their citizens is uninformed and open to distortions of what is true. Libraries are discarding much of their print collections, often without concern to sustainability. Who will be holding the last copy? Who will commit to permanently retaining all the print materials acquired by them?

With the publication explosion in the 1950's and 1960's Libraries undertook the role of archivist with the agreement of the publisher. Libraries collected and collected. They maintained strong bibliographic control over their collections. They improved the development of great standards for bibliographic control through the power of the MARC record.

With the substantive growth of digital publishing publishers took control again of the decisions as to what they should digitise and also how they would make that material available archivally. We are yet to see the net situation emerge as we move from paper to digital. We are yet to understand how to make our collections sustainable and to ensure to all worthwhile materials are preserved, as much of that earlier material will not be digitised. The business case for this new situation is yet to be detailed but much has happened and this book of essays seeks to explain that which is happening in many parts of our world.

The Repositories are constantly evolving their policies in response to altered circumstances. Many are evaluating their foundational collecting policies which

---

1 https://www.nature.com/articles/d41586-017-07817-1

may have been as simple as 'taking everything offered by member libraries' or more complex policies dealing with local circumstances and politics. In evaluating these policies there is an effort to more strongly to direct what is being collected rather than a simple responsive posture. In this there can be a consideration of collaborative catalogues across repositories in different places which might lead to a de-duplicating policies between these collections.

Many of these issues are being explored in this book. The plethora of possibilities and nuanced responses mean that this volume is not only interesting but vital. As a matter of critical public policy there needs to be a future focused approach recognising the importance and value of our cultural and social heritage. A failure to do so will result in huge gaps; a barren desert of what was once the rich and vital intellectual life of our societies.

Steve O'Connor

2 Re-visiting the concept and purpose of the print repository

All things change. A sage said that the only constant we have in our lives is change! How we perceive that change happening, or even if we do perceive that change is both a reflection of our experience and also our openness to the rate of change. We can sometimes be too close to an event, a landscape or an issue to be hardly aware of any changes even seismic ones. This is a major difficulty when we are planning for the future and we can hardly see the changes which have been happening around us.

This chapter seeks to deal with our perspectives on the many changes happening around publishing, particularly of books and the impact of the Repository Library. The impacts include the recent past, decisions made and more importantly what the future might hold for these and new repositories.

Change is the vapour affecting this chapter and also the salutary lesson that we need to re-examine what is around us. We do not need to do this everyday but we need to be mindful that our gaze is not blinkered by focusing on the day-to-day activities and the steady middle markings on the highway we are travelling on. As professionals we need to be adjusting the horizon constantly and assimilating changes in our environment to understand their impact, but more importantly, the potential impact. In particular we need to constantly see ourselves not as 'insiders' but as 'outsiders'. We need binoculars so that we can see as far down the highway as is reasonable but also have 'fish-eye' lenses which enable us to see the happenings in the periphery of our vision. Both are important. The long view and also the fish eye view. Armed with these two views we can then begin to analyse what we should be focusing on in our planning.

This chapter is making the case that Print Repositories have made a significant contribution to the preservation and retention of our cultural heritage as expressed in the print culture. They have been embraced as an essential unit in the library and information architecture. I would argue however that rarely have we seen Repositories as being central to library operations and capabilities. Not much serious thought has gone into what has been happening over the past 30 years; that we have rested on our laurels without growing the concept. There has been little evolution; rather there has been stagnation. Not stagnation of operations and excellence but of impact thinking. This is the absence of thinking about the relevance of the existing corpus of collected materials and future collecting; it is the absence of an integrated architecture for print and digital.

https://doi.org/10.1515/9783110535372-002

They do not exist in isolation of each other but we have been treating them in that way. Our thinking has been focused on what we have been collecting, not why we are collecting it. Most often we have been focusing on the retention of content at an institutional level. There are notable exceptions to this of course but the collecting has been on what is given to us in the Repository, not on what we should be collecting; not on what we need to collect at an institutional level or even at a collaborative level.

Clearly what we thought we were good at once is not necessarily what we are or will be good at in the future. The argument here is that change is always with us but that the strategic view in which repositories were established has largely changed and not in the manner which was originally understood. We are strategically dreaming. We need to step outside the confines of our existing thinking and look at what it could be, what it should be. It is not likely to be what it is now; it is definitely not what we started out to achieve.

A limited view of the landscape

Even a few short years ago, we perceived that e-books were the thing of the future and that the print book was totally passé! Many library colleagues have worked hard to diminish their collections, their research collections in anticipation that they would be digitised and/or that someone else would have collected the items and/or would retain those items. No guarantees. It is now clear from the evidence that the progress or take-up of e-books has stalled and that the law on copyright has, understandably, been slow in asserting the legal realities of this new world. The 'right' of the researcher/student to use print books and their content has not been replicated in the digital world. Yet, the publishing world has quickly realised that the new operating digital environment has enabled new licensing conditions and, of course, new income streams. Publishing Houses now have two income streams for print and for digital. This is not a bad thing for the publishers but a smart one adapting to the changed conditions.

The unit sale of print books has in 2016 risen by 3.3% for the third year in a row[1]. On the other hand the trade sales of e-books fell by 15% in 2015 over the previous year[2]. The sale of e-books in the UK fell by 17% in 2016 while the sales

---

1 http://www.publishersweekly.com/pw/by-topic/industry-news/bookselling/article/72450-print-book-sales-rose-again-in-2016.html
2 http://www.publishersweekly.com/pw/by-topic/digital/retailing/article/70696-as-e-book-sales-decline-digital-fatigue-grows.html

of print books increased by 8% for the same period. Overall digital journals grew by 1.7% in the same period.[3] Some are saying that it is 'digital fatigue'. I am aware of a strong move in libraries across the globe to literally dump books from their collections being convinced that print books were an old and no longer valued artifact of value. Perhaps this was a shallow conclusion. A conclusion however with a lasting impact. This is not to ascribe blame to any actions but to highlight a story of what has been happening over the past 20 to 30 years and the way in which the various threads to this story have come together to create a new fabric. My local university, and many like it, just wheeled books out of the door with scant regard to the value of those books or the special collections which had been formed. They were driven by mindless statements that everything is on the internet, so why retain it, and, by the way, I want the library spaces for other purposes. So the management edict from on high was given effect by a lack of understanding and thinking in the library. The value of having books on a physical shelf or even in local storage is far more valuable than the loss of burying it in the local garbage dump.

Over the past ten years there has been a battle in the American Courts between the American Society of Authors and Google regarding the legal position of scanned books in Google Books. Google had arrived at the position with its system Google Books whereby authors searching for a particular title were able to view snippets of the book. The Society of Authors felt that this was impinging on their members' capability to earn income. The American courts in April 2016[4] indicated that the 'Fair Use' doctrine allowed the 20 million scanned books by Google to be displayed across the internet but only as a sampler, so to speak. Users can see only short grabs of the text but can purchase the book through various suppliers or purchase e-access through Google Books. The resolution of what the law means in these new circumstances has taken a long time to happen. The impact on libraries remains to be fully seen. Some have argued that this allows libraries not to collect those items for their users. If this were the case, then every time a particular title is required by a user, another charge has to be made, this time to Google Books. Under the previous paradigm the 'library purchased copy' of a title would be available for multiple accesses at no additional cost.

The significance of this legal position is nuanced. On the one hand it demonstrates the power of new technologies to make available abundant

---

3 https://www.theguardian.com/books/2017/apr/27/screen-fatigue-sees-uk-ebook-sales-plunge-17-as-readers-return-to-print
4 https://www.copyright.com.au/2016/04/us-authors-guilds-review-google-books-case-denied/

amounts of traditional information in the form of published books. Of course this is a good thing. But it is a form of apartheid. The more that people have to pay for their reading, the more we will have a tranche of our population not being able to be information literate because they have the disposable income. If users of our libraries and repositories are unable to seek and read information freely, then our society has a serious problem. The quotation attributed to Thomas Jefferson that 'Information is the currency of democracy' is clearly a rallying call for libraries and repositories. Libraries in this regard can be seen to be abrogating their responsibility for free and open access to information through their institutions. They are being sold on the idea that technology is unstintingly 'a good', whereas it is truer to say that technology is not Manichean in itself but rather finds value in what uses it is put to. Intrinsically, 'Technology' has no good or evil value in itself so to draw the conclusion that anything piece of technology has to be better than a 'non-technology' such as print books is simply wrong.

This is clearly a cursory look at what has happened with little overview of the institutional response to these circumstances.

> *"While academic libraries in the United States have actively collaborated with each other for more than 100 years, the digital turn has brought an explosion of interest in and pursuit of cross-institutional collaboration. These include large-scale digital access and preservation initiatives like HathiTrust, print preservation and access collaborations like Scholar's Trust and WEST, metropolitan-level efforts ranging broadly from the Chicago Collections Alliance to MARLI, unmediated borrowing such as ConnectNY, and, of burgeoning strategic importance, the collaborations enabled through cloud-based library services platforms for consortia and systems like Orbis Cascade. These models differ broadly, as do their impact and prospects, but the level of interest and investment is undeniable"[5].*

The ithaka report's author Christine Wolff-Eisenberg further indicates: "Across institution types, library leaders report spending less than 10% of their time on this type of activity. These directors tend to spend the greatest share of their time on administrative and leadership duties, including those related to budgeting, staffing, and management."[6] This report further highlights the percentages of academic libraries working collaboratively with shared off-site collections and other services.

> *"How important are the following types of collaborative agreements with other libraries, established through bilateral agreements, library systems, or consortia?"[7]*

---

5 http://www.sr.ithaka.org/blog/why-libraries-collaborate/
6 http://www.sr.ithaka.org/blog/why-libraries-collaborate/
7 http://www.sr.ithaka.org/blog/why-libraries-collaborate/

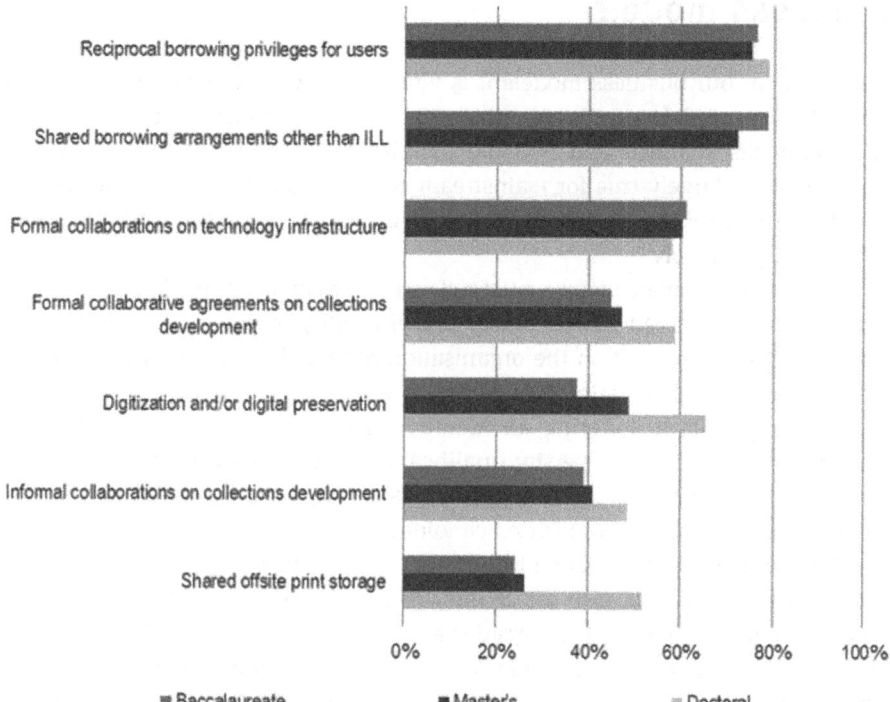

Figure 2.1: Percentage of respondents who indicated that each is very important.

The emphases in the American collaboration scene are an interesting reflection for the broader set of Repository managers. Shared off site print storage at the resource-intensive libraries is very important, but is so much more important when combined with formal collaborations with technology, digital preservation as well as formal and informal collection development efforts. It is mainly the larger or doctoral producing institutions that have the interest in each of these areas. Any view of these overlapping areas of interest can begin the process of service development of new business model opportunities. The sole focus on the existing business model, if maintained, will inevitably create a role which is limiting into the future. The existing role is important but will never lead the profession as it should or could. It will never allow the Repositories to gain a mainstream and strong role in how libraries do operate. It will never allow them to fulfill a necessary complimentary and value-adding role.

Business models

Reflecting on our business models it is vital to think about what we are doing and why we are doing it. The argument of this chapter has been thus far that the world has changed and that the popular conception that everything has gone digital is largely true for mainstream academic journals but not for monographs. In fact print monographs or books are being published and sold more often than previously.

The whole strategic picture must reflect that which is happening in the institutions who are served by the library and if at all possible anticipate the new situation. This is to position the organisation not for the present but the future. The pressures on academic libraries are to reflect a higher education environment which is itself suffering an identity crisis. Many major companies are openly indicating that university qualifications are no longer an employment pre-requisite. Companies like Penguin are saying that they "wanted to open up opportunities to attract more varied candidates into publishing, an industry that has been criticised for its lack of diversity"[8] while Ernst Young[9] are expressing similar views. Will this also affect the qualification demands for professional librarians? At another level universities are seeking to reduce their costs and, at the same time, increasing their relevance to time-poor student populations. They are achieving this by offering their courses in digital form. The readings for students are limited to digital articles for the most part and very little reliance on 'browsing library shelves for relevant content'. Shelf capacity in the library has been removed and replaced by more and more study spaces for students. The space ratios of books to study desks have now been completely reversed. This requires off-site storage or the simpler methodology consigning these tomes to the dust bins and garbage tips.

Repositories generally have been exceptional successes as operations being led and supported by the profession. The profession however has always seen the 'library' as being the strategic centre and that repositories have been at the extremity or as a 'service-forgotten'. Except for the very largest institutions the repository models have been cooperative or collaborative but always limited by non-compete clauses. In other words, libraries have exhibited management behaviour models which have found the collaborative management behaviour models as being too difficult and have therefore been left untried. In these circumstances, it has always been preferable to remain in a single hierarchical

---

8 https://www.theguardian.com/books/2016/jan/18/penguin-ditches-the-need-for-job-seekers-to-have-university-degrees
9 http://www.huffingtonpost.co.uk/2016/01/07/ernst-and-young-removes-degree-classification-entry-criteria_n_7932590.html

management model. Perhaps this is no longer how management should behave. Are libraries to be managed wholly within their own institutional boundaries. This paper argues that there are a good number of collaborative management areas which could add real value to student and researcher service need.

New business models such as these suggest futures that elevate collaborative behaviours. The diagram below which was provided by OCLC research efforts highlights how access to content has and is changing even further. The key points here are that access has shifted largely from owned content to facilitated content. Yet the usage rates of collaborative repositories remains stubbornly at less than 1 or 2% annually. Research also reveals that the content used in one year from a repository is not that which is used in the following year. In other words the use of a repository can be relatively high but over a longer period. The content is valued and used. There is a demand for this lower use material. For this reason, we need to be focusing on marketing the sizeable amounts of content in our repositories into the global environment. This requires a shift of management thinking about our repositories in that the content can be discovered in a global environment and delivered in the same manner.

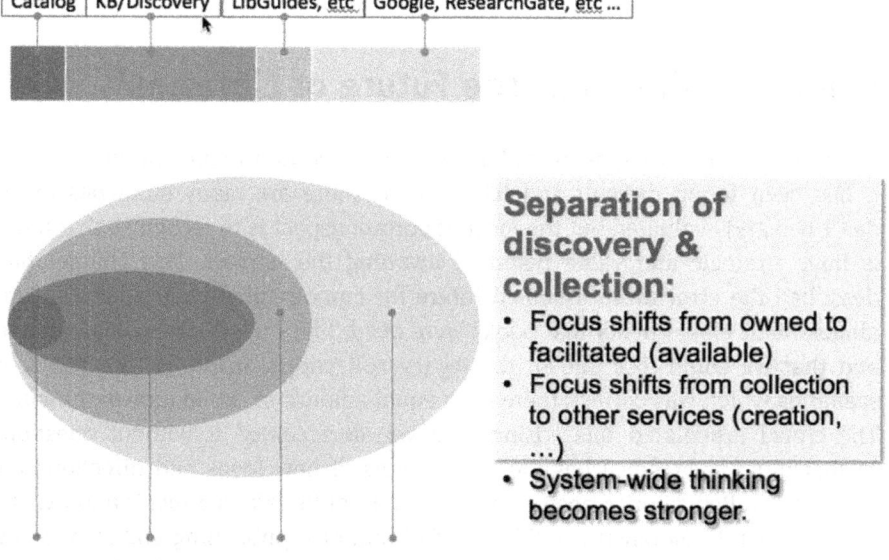

Fig. 2.2: Separation of discovery & collection.

The economics of individual institutional repositories are more costly than that of collaborative or cooperative repositories. There are limited studies revealing the extent of overlap between these collaborative repositories. There are really no collection development policies for these repositories or certainly for a range of connected repositories. The development of areas of strength for collaborative repositories would be a one smart direction in which to head. It would, for instance, be logical for the National Repository Library of Finland to be a source of lesser known and used materials from that whole region; a research centre integrating with research libraries across the globe.

Repositories standing alone, yet together

It was noted earlier in this chapter that collaborative behaviours are being actively pursued in the area of collection building and sharing, especially in the research environments.[10] The research treasures locked up in our repositories need to be unleashed for discovery into the global content market place. The various repositories across the globe can work together themselves to ensure that their efforts are focused and coordinated.

Wei Lai Tushuguan 'The Future of Libraries'

The full potential of Repositories has not been tried and found wanting. Rather it has been found difficult and left untried. There are many strategies to be described and evaluated but the most important aspect is to recognise that there is huge strategic and value potential awaiting the harvest. This chapter has described the error of an assumed future for monographs where there was an almost blind global belief that books were dead, that only digital would survive and that we could toss out all the legacy collections. In all of that series of scenarios which was correct, there is an equal amount of 'blind crowd' thinking. The crowd articulated this 'vision' and we all accepted it without question. In that blind acceptance lies the many germs of new ideas and directions for repositories. Repositories need to be tried and not be left as difficult and dying.

    The past developments of this world of libraries, publishing and technology have not been linear. There has not been a linear path of development to

---

10 http://www.sr.ithaka.org/blog/why-libraries-collaborate/

this present. There will not be a linear path to the future. The future will be disjointed with decision points, new paths, and new directions. In that uncertainty lies many exciting possibilities for imaginations to grasp and to drive. The foundations of repositories is well laid and solid. The cooperative or collaborative repositories have fertile ground in which to sow many new futures. Be brave! Be Bold!

Alasdair Ball and Liz White
3 Managing complex collections in an interconnected world

The British Library is one of the world's greatest libraries, holding over 150 million physical items and billions of pages of web content. We are the proud custodians of one of the richest heritage collections anywhere, including international treasures from the Diamond Sutra to the Mewar Ramayana as well as many of the UK's most significant riches including two of the four surviving 1215 Magna Carta and the Lindisfarne Gospels. Our oldest collection items are three millennia old Chinese Oracle Bones and every day half a terabyte of new digital content is added to the collection. The perspective offered by these earliest attempts at writing, and the whole span of human communication and thought in between, gives us a rare perspective on managing complex collections in an interconnected world, spanning texts in every known written language as well as AV material, web and data.

Added to this, the British Library itself is a surprisingly young institution, formed in 1973 and a near-contemporary of Microsoft and Apple. As our 'Living Knowledge' vision asserts, the Library was born out of a courageous post-war vision to create a new kind of national institution, directly in the service of research and innovation. At its heart were and are the matchless collections inherited from the Library of the British Museum. But the genius of the Library's founders was to combine that Enlightenment heritage with a determination to keep pace with science and research in all its forms, supporting and underpinning the whole ecology of information services in the UK.

The challenges of managing complex collections in a digital world have been at the heart of our strategy development over the past decade. Published in 2010, our 2020 Vision noted the following drivers:
- The pace of technological changes
- The growing expectations of digital service quality among researchers and information users
- An increasing proliferation of collaborative research models

More recently, as we scoped our current Living Knowledge Vision, five other major strategic drivers were identified:
- A revolution in the creation, analysis and exploitation of **data** in all its forms, from the vast scientific and social datasets typically badged as 'big data', to innovations derived from digitised cultural content. This has led to new ways for the British Library to use its exponentially growing collections

https://doi.org/10.1515/9783110535372-003

of both historic digitised content and born-digital content, as well as new challenges ahead for librarianship, digital storage and access. During this period, British Library staff began to develop new and emerging professional roles as creators and analysers of new datasets; as experts in setting standards (improving data and enabling links in a complex digital landscape) and as a centre for cross-disciplinary working and business innovation in librarianship and curation.

–   At the same time, the idea of **openness**, in multiple ways, had a profound effect on the landscape of information services and cultural provision. Indeed, more than 25 million images were made available under open license terms by the British Library between 2012 and 2015. The Open Data movement began to unlock publicly-held information for analysis and re-use by researchers, businesses and the public. In academic research, the scientific community continued working through the complex process of making research data open and accessible. Open Access to research publications developed faster and more extensively than many envisaged, with growing volumes of publicly funded research made available openly on the web. And the theme had a social and ethical dimension too, with a growing consensus on the need for arts and cultural institutions to make their collections and activities open and accessible to everyone across the UK, whatever their social background or geographical location.

–   Related to this we saw a growing interest in, and understanding of, the importance of **creativity and culture** as contributors to economic growth and wellbeing. Major recent programmes of study into the idea of cultural value – supported by, among others, the University of Warwick (2015)[1] and the Arts & Humanities Research Council (2015)[2] – explored the systemic links between the provision of arts and culture and the wider health of society and the economy. The launch of the Creative Industries Federation signalled a new confidence from the arts and creative sector in asserting its role at the heart of the UK's industrial strategy.

–   Evidence from our visitor surveys suggests that, at a time when the provision of knowledge and culture is increasingly digital and screen-based, the value and importance of high-quality **physical spaces** was growing, not diminishing, as was the perceived value of real human encounters and physical artefacts. For libraries in particular this means that there is no simple cost-saving 'switch-out' from physical estates to digital platforms: our users require continued investment in both, and success in each realm feeds interest in the other.

---

1 http://www2.warwick.ac.uk/research/warwickcommission/futureculture/finalreport/
warwick_commission_final_report.pdf

2 http://www.ahrc.ac.uk/documents/publications/cultural-value-project-final-report/

Published in January 2015, *Living Knowledge: The British Library 2015–2023* set out our ambition to be the most open, creative and innovative institution of its kind by the time of its 50th anniversary in 2023 and restated our mission to make our intellectual heritage available to everyone, for research, inspiration and enjoyment. Living Knowledge also introduced a guiding framework of 6 core purposes:

Custodianship – We build, curate and preserve the UK's national collection of published, written and digital content

Research – We support and stimulate research of all kinds

Business – We help businesses to innovate and grow

Culture – We engage everyone with memorable cultural experiences

Learning – We inspire young people and learners of all ages

International – We work with partners around the world to advance knowledge and mutual understanding.

In 2016 we launched the "Living Knowledge Network", a new pilot project, supported by Arts Council England and based around partnership working with the public library sector as well as the National Library of Scotland and National Library of Wales. Our vision is of a mutually supportive network of major libraries, who share our ambition to be open, creative and innovative and who are willing to combine collective strengths to deliver engaging services at local, regional and national level. The "Living Knowledge Network" will combine the best of the British Library and our national collection with the expertise and reach of those city libraries that are already working at scale and transforming their services and spaces through innovation.

Custodianship is the British Library's first and core purpose, the one on which all the others depend. The British Library Act 1972 exhorts us to be 'comprehensive', and unlike a museum collection, ours grows all the time: each month, by approximately 0.8 kilometres of new physical items, and around ten terabytes of new digital content. Exact assessments of the current scale of the collection are hard to make: varying definitions of the word "item" yield varying estimates of between 150 million and 200 million items, including books, journals, newspapers, patents, maps, prints, manuscripts, stamps, photographs, sound recordings, digital publications of all kinds and over 7 billion pages of UK web content.

One of the most significant developments between 2011 and 2015 was the Legal Deposit Libraries (Non-Print Works) Regulations 2013, enabling the UK's Legal Deposit Libraries to collect digital material for the first time. Since then, we have been working in partnership with the National Libraries of Scotland and Wales and the Libraries of the Universities of Oxford, Cambridge and Trinity College Dublin to collect the UK and Ireland's output of born-digital content, including the entire UK web. An article entitled "Observations on the development of non-print legal deposit in the UK" was published in Library Review, Vol. 61 Iss: 5, pp. 362–377[3]

As custodians of one of the largest cultural heritage collections in the world, we are challenged to manage a highly complex mix of physical and digital artefacts. Preserving and providing long-term access to these invaluable assets is a huge and ever more complex challenge, and one the British Library is required to tackle through the duties conferred in the British Library Act of 1972. These challenges range from the fundamental storage facilities required to meet our statutory custodianship obligations, through digitising cultural content at scale, to developing the skills required to remain a global leader. In order to fulfil this mission the British Library is globally recognised as a genuine leader in the field of collection management.

As a legal deposit library, a copy of every UK print publication must be given by its publishers to the British Library. The extension of the Act to cover digitally published material extends our scope so that we now provide the shared digital infrastructure used by all six UK legal deposit libraries[4]. In addition to Legal Deposit, the Library receives a significant proportion of overseas titles distributed in the UK, and has an on-going programme for content acquisitions. As a result, the Library has extensive collections from many countries, in many languages and in many formats, both print and digital: books, manuscripts, journals, newspapers, magazines, sound and music recordings, videos, play-scripts, patents, databases, maps, stamps, prints and drawings. Our collections continue to grow rapidly, with around 8km of print and 150Tb of digital content being added each year, creating continual demands for physical and digital storage space.

The increasingly eclectic mix of digital and analogue content within our collections makes significant demands on the Collection Management function from a structural, process and skills perspective. In response to these demands

---

3 Richard Gibby, Caroline Brazier, "Observations on the development of non-print legal deposit in the UK", Library Review, Vol. 61 Iss: 5, pp. 362–377: http://www.emeraldinsight.com/doi/full/10.1108/00242531211280487

4 The British Library; The University Library, Cambridge; The Bodleian Libraries, Oxford; The National Library of Scotland; The National Library of Wales; The Library of Trinity College, Dublin

there has been, over the past decade or so, a gradual transition in organisational structure from a classical library model focusing on our own physical collections, to a more fluid set of structures and processes addressing the challenges of managing complex combinations of physical and digital content. Simultaneously, there has been a requirement for Collection Management to support the more outward-facing profile of the wider organisation. Table 1 provides an overview of this progression.

Table 1 infers two drivers which are influencing our approach to collection management. The first relates to the boundaries that we apply when thinking about managing collections. We have moved from an internal focus on managing our own holdings, to increasingly linking out to other trusted institutions to identify relevant content and to share, where rights permit, access. This change affects the entire content lifecycle. It influences our approach to content acquisition and licensing, metadata creation and systems design. Positioning ourselves within the wider information landscape also reinforces the need for common standards and wider interoperability.

The second driver, that also broadens the traditional scope of collection management, is in supporting the strategic remit of the Library in its engagement across a wider, and more diverse, set of audiences. Given that custodianship of the collections is the core mandate of the Collection Management function, we need to balance the imperative to enable wider access whilst also ensuring that appropriate control systems to safeguard our collections are well embedded.

As the proportion of digital content increases across collections, opportunities arise for designing wider sectoral solutions to shared information management challenges. Digital collections display more uniformity than that seen in traditional physical collections where manuscripts, archives, philatelic, cartographic and printed collections present unique and distinctive challenges. Whether a digital artefact is a web page, a digitised object, or an e-book, they are all, at one level, a collection of digital files that require description, preservation and access. Although this clearly over-simplifies the diversity of digital content, there are a number of shared opportunities, particularly in the area of repository management, where there is significant potential for collaboration across institutions.

These opportunities are further facilitated by the ease with which digital collections can be managed over a network of geographically dispersed members. The network can allow individual participants to retain control whilst, at the same time, enabling services to be created based on shared infrastructure. This not only offers the potential for improved user services, based on a wider, shared,

Table 1

	Collection Management Organisational Structure	Content Profile	Network Engagement	Solutions Development	Organisational Orientation	Organisational Priorities
2005–2010	Classical, functional design	Vast, historic, physical collections; Contemporary publishing primarily in print form	Strong technical network of national libraries; well embedded relationships with research and HE	Off-the-shelf, integrated, library management solutions replacing legacy fragmented architecture	Primarily internally focused	Advocacy for non-print regulations
2010–2015	Based around organisation of content lifecycle; integrated end-to-end workflow design	Introduction of non-print legal deposit increases volumes of digital content; growth of digitisation for commercial and preservation purposes	Emergent collaborative initiatives with HE such as the UK Research Reserve (UKRR)	Internal development of digital solutions to augment existing library management systems.	Collection Management primarily internally focused; Wider organisation more outward and audience facing	Cost control in response to funding pressures; redefinition of organisational purposes and values
2015–	Growth in digital content processing and Digital Preservation resources; External engagement agenda (loans, exhibitions, digitisation) requires increasing Collection Management support.	Scale of digital ingest increases, but print volumes not reducing at the expected rate; increasing diversity of digital publishing; Large digitisation initiatives	Increasingly outward facing and cross-cultural; increasing engagement with cross-domain institutions in areas such as rights management and persistent identifiers	Emergence of off-the-shelf systems to manage highly scaled digital collections. In-house development focused on both internal integration as well as multi-tenancy solutions to support wider sectors	Increasingly outward facing and cross domain; Increased international engagement in both library and cultural sectors	Development of major portfolios to support purposes and strategy; wider and more sophisticated service propositions; inclusion and diversity; skills development

corpus of digital content, but also enables a reduction in overall network costs through economies of scale in procurement and development.

Whilst digital collections offer opportunities for shared endeavour, organisations also face common challenges in unlocking their rich physical collections to a user base whose expectation is that content will be available on-line. The large scale digitisation of artefacts enables this, and institutions across the world are investing in building capability in this area. The British Library is no exception and has a number of on-going partnerships, including:

- DC Thompson FindMyPast. This aims to digitise 40 million pages of newsprint by 2020 and to make them available via both the on-line British Newspaper Archive, as well as in our own reading rooms.
- The Qatar Foundation to make newly digitised content relating to the Gulf region available online for the first time, predominantly from the Library's India Office Records archive. By early 2017, the Qatar Digital Library has been viewed by just under half a million users from 222 countries.
- The National Library of Israel which has yielded 68,000 pages of the Library's Hebrew Manuscripts collection.
- The Bibliothèque Nationale de France (generously funded by the Polonsky Foundation), to digitise 800 illuminated manuscripts from the period 700–1200, making them available online for the first time.
- The *Two Centuries of Indian Print* project, which is seeking to digitise thousands of early printed South Asian language books dating from 1713–1914.

These large scale digitisation initiatives create and sustain an increasing demand for digital infrastructure. The artefacts created by digitisation require active management and, in some cases, long term preservation. In addition, born-digital content is becoming increasingly complex, with publications containing text, audio and video components. Add to this the potential demand to preserve the underlying datasets of research outputs and a complex set of challenges begins to emerge. Addressing these challenges will rely on both expertise and the ability to operate at significant scale. It is potentially not attractive to many (particular smaller) organisations to invest in these systems and skill sets and, given the potential benefits of collaborative working outlined earlier, it is likely that there will be movement towards consortial and partnership arrangements in this area. These wider arrangements may not even be sector specific, and national institutions such as The British Library, could potentially play a convening role across domains including culture, HE and the wider library network.

Expertise in managing large collections of print based materials is traditionally well embedded in information organisations. The challenge here is to

Figure 1: The British Library in Boston Spa, Yorkshire (Photo © Kippa Matthews).

develop innovative solutions which reduce costs or allow repurposing of space for other activities. This needs to be achieved whist still retaining timely access to (often low use) material for research purposes. Increasingly, organisations are considering the opportunities for collaboration in this area. Exemplars include the Research Collections and Preservation Consortium (ReCAP[5]) facility in the USA and the United Kingdom Research Reserve (UKRR[6]) in the UK. The latter enabled nearly 100km of space to be released across 29 Higher Education institutions through a partnership between universities and The British Library.

The challenges of physical storage are also being addressed through the uptake of new storage technologies. As an example, 2014 saw the completion of a new newspaper repository at The British Library in Boston Spa, Yorkshire (Figures 1 and 2). Holding more than 53,000 separate news titles and more than 700 million pages of newsprint dating back to the 16th Century, the BL's collections are vast. Saving the collection for posterity included a move from the Colindale site in North London (a 1930s building with no environmental controls)

5 https://recap.princeton.edu/
6 http://www.ukrr.ac.uk/

Figure 2: The British Library in Boston Spa, Yorkshire (Photo © Kippa Matthews).

to a new high density, low oxygen, automated store in Boston Spa. Funded by a major capital investment from the department of Culture, Media and Sport, it is able to house the growing collection in temperature and humidity controlled conditions to internationally agreed standards.

Increasingly, the trends identified in relation to collection management are reflected in other aspects of the British Library's core purposes. Digital partnerships have enabled us to share content and reach new audiences at scale, such as the partnership with DC Thompson FindMyPast, which will enable us to digitise 40m pages of newsprint by 2020 and to make them available via the British Newspaper Archive. Likewise, the "Two Centuries of Indian Print" project is a partnership between the British Library, the School of Cultural Texts and Records (SCTR) of Jadavpur University, Srishti Institute of Art, Design and Technology, and the Library at SOAS University of London, working with the National Library of India, the National Mission on Libraries, and other institutions in India[7]

During the initial phase, this partnership will see 1,000 rare Bengali printed books and 3,000 early printed books digitised, as well as the catalogue records

---

7 See more at: https://www.bl.uk/projects/two-centuries-of-indian-print#sthash.rgon4Oqm.dpuf

enhanced in order to facilitate automated searching and aid discovery by researchers. As with other mass digitisation projects, we expect increased digital content to continue to drive physical visits too, supporting the British Library's overarching aim to make our intellectual content available to everyone for research, inspiration and enjoyment.

Wolfgang Mayer and Brigitte Kromp
4 Shared Archiving Austria

A Joint Archiving Strategy for Austrian University Libraries

The Starting point

One characteristic of the Austrian university landscape is that infrastructure and research at Austrian universities are mainly funded by state institutions and public money. With 8.4 million inhabitants, Austria has 22 state universities with around 308.700 students, 21 universities of applied sciences with 48.000 students and 13 private universities with 10.200 students.[1]

By passing the Universities Act 2002, all Austrian universities have become autonomous legal bodies in terms of their financial and administrative matters.[2] One of the consequences of this autonomy is that ministries no longer provide any central money to university libraries. Another consequence is that no central office has been installed responsible for cross-institutional library projects such as shared archiving or planning and building joint deposit libraries. Thus, university libraries can only address their own university rectorates in terms of budgetary requests. In addition, applying for third-party funds in the academic library landscape has little tradition and therefore does not have a significant impact on library budgets.

In order to be able to provide for the least necessary cooperation, 14 university libraries founded the Austrian Academic Library Consortium (Kooperation E-Medien Österreich, KEMÖ) on July 1st 2005 with the purpose to jointly license and acquire electronic media. The consortium has since then grown steadily with now 58 members, among them 18 university libraries.[3] As many of the consortial licenses for electronic journals were based on the print subscriptions of the participating libraries, it can be assumed that these printed holdings are extensive and in part available at many libraries. This fact is also relevant for the project Shared Archiving Austria.

---

1 uni:data : Data Warehouse Higher Education Sector (http://www.bmwfw.gv.at/unidata; last view on June 14th, 2017)
2 Federal Act on the Organisation of Universities and their Studies (Universities Act 2002 – UG) (http://www.ris.bka.gv.at/GeltendeFassung.wxe?Abfrage=Bundesnormen&Gesetzesnummer= 20002128; last view on December 13th, 2017)
3 Official website of Kooperation E-Medien Österreich (https://konsortien.at/; version of December 13th, 2017)

https://doi.org/10.1515/9783110535372-004

Pilot phase

On the basis of the framework conditions mentioned before, two similar initiatives were started in 2010 independent of each other. The Council of Austrian University Libraries (Forum der Universitätsbibliotheken Österreichs, ubifo[4]) implemented a focus group called „National Archiving Concept" in order to elaborate a theoretical concept on this topic. At the same time Vienna University Library started a project to eliminate duplicate items held by its then around 50 sub-libraries. In order to avoid working parallel on the same topic and to pool competences it was decided to merge the two projects.

For the purpose of their cooperation the two groups agreed on the following common understanding of "shared archiving": Only one item of printed journals where the journal is also available electronically is kept in Austria; multiple items can be removed from the inventory. The underlying idea of this concept is to determine a "best portfolio", and to assign it to selected archiving libraries.

Instead of laying down an exact definition, it was decided to create a catalogue of criteria to define a best portfolio. These criteria are: maximum completeness, good state of preservation and quick availability of the printed items. The simplest case of a best portfolio could for example be the portfolio of a single institution or it is generated by combining hitherto incomplete portfolios. The principle of shared archiving though allows that a best portfolio is maintained by different libraries at different locations. However, if libraries hand over their items, they also hand over ownership of these items.

This way of joint acting is to provide for an equal burden sharing. The corresponding archiving library commits itself to abide by agreed standards such as timely document delivery and appropriate long-term preservation. The other partner libraries are able to reduce the cost of floor space and administration by reducing or even removing completely their duplicates.

An organisation team installed by ubifo set up two task forces in order to make these ideas become reality:

- The task force "Contract Drafting" was responsible for preparing a contract for participating universities which on the one hand provides for the necessary legal framework for this cooperation, but on the other hand allows for enough scope in terms of the operational implementation to react to future ideas and plans.
- On the basis of a typical journals package the task force "Workflow" had to define a standardised workflow which can serve as role model for future projects. The journals package of the American Chemical Society (ACS) was chosen as suitable pilot project.

---

4 Official website of ubifo (http://ubifo.at/; last view on December 13th, 2017)

The decisive criteria to choose ACS for the pilot were:
- a manageable number of titles – however with complex publication histories;
- electronic availability of all journals including far-reaching back years;
- few participating partners due to the subject-specific focus (only twelve university libraries with subscriptions);
- common interest due to consortial licensing.

Both task forces carried out the pilot project in 2011 and delivered a joint report which showed that it was possible to remove at least 860 linear meters covered by ACS printed journals in Austrian university libraries by removing all multiple printed journal issues. In terms of floor space, this corresponds to 116 square meters, according to the DIN technical report 13[5]. Taking into account a monthly rental rate[6] of €13.91 per square meter it is possible to save rental costs of €19,363 per year; this money could for example be invested in collection development.

Libraries acting as archiving libraries do without the maximum gain of floor space reduction, but have the advantage of sharpening their collection profiles, gaining prestige and thus securing their sites.

As a first immediate quality improvement for library users, all catalogue entries and holdings for all ACS journals were reviewed, corrected if needed, and enriched by adding so far not catalogued electronic holdings (e.g. supplements). 387 university library holdings were found pertaining to the 58 ACS journal titles in the Austrian Union Catalogue. Of these 387 holdings, 97 had to be corrected extensively following review by the university libraries and 43 had to be deleted because there were no longer any holdings.

Start of real operation

The concept of Shared Archiving Austria was laid down on the basis of the results mentioned before. In 2012 the necessary legal documents were formalised including a framework agreement (the general cooperation agreement) plus potential addenda (the individual product agreements) and the cooperation agreement was signed by all state universities. The first individual product agreement on shared archiving of the printed journals of the American Physical Society (APS) was signed in 2013.

---

5 DIN Technical Report 13 (2009), p 36, table 13, consecutive number 2
6 Average rental price of the complete floor space rented by Vienna University including operating costs 2011

Contract formalisation

The legal framework of Shared Archiving Austria is set up in a way to enable as many universities as possible to sign the slim framework agreement that stipulates the rights and responsibilities of the archiving libraries next to the usual general terms and conditions. In addition, individual product agreements for each archived product (can be single publishers, collections or something similar) are set up, but are signed only by those libraries participating in the shared archiving of these journals.

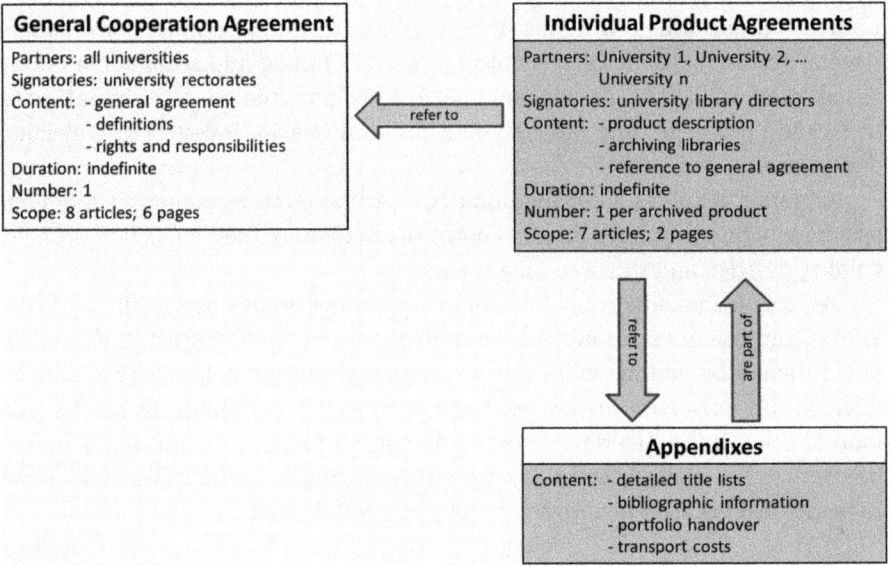

Figure 4.1: Contract architecture.

The general cooperation agreement is signed by the university rectorates, whereas the university library directors are responsible for the operative implementation and signing of the individual product agreements.

In order to convince as many institutions as possible to take part in shared archiving and to avoid disadvantages for library users, the task force identified the following relevant topics:

Content of the General Cooperation Agreement (excerpts)

Article 1 Subject matter of the agreement

According to the terms and conditions of this agreement, the subject matter is the shared archiving of printed journal holdings available at the cooperation partners and to make available state-wide one archiving copy of each printed journal available. It is stated explicitly that notwithstanding the foregoing each university library or their sub-libraries can archive printed journals.

Article 2 Contractual services of the cooperation partners
Rights and responsibilities of the archiving library:

∴ Complete item records in catalogues / search engines

"Complete and current entry and update of records in a central catalogue": The archiving library has to label its archived material as such in the Austrian Union Catalogue in order to make publicly visible its responsibilities resulting from the general cooperation agreement (e.g. document delivery).

∴ Document delivery to the participating partners

"Delivery of required articles as needed to participating libraries": In spite of the fact that document delivery should only be necessary in exceptional cases due to the electronic availability of the content, it was considered essential to define clear rules for mutual document delivery. It was defined as service standard that each required article has to be delivered electronically with 24 hours by the archiving library.

∴ Long-term preservation and careful storage

"Long-term preservation and careful storage": Each archiving library is obliged to undertake all reasonable efforts to maintain the printed material assigned.

∴ Information of partners in case of plans to dissolve a portfolio

"Information of partners in case of plans to dissolve a portfolio": In order to avoid adding responsibilities to the contract which would make it impossible for universities to participate, regulations what should happen if a portfolio was to be dissolved were taken up in the contract. The archiving library has to inform all libraries participating in the respective product agreement timely if it plans to dissolve the printed items assigned. Therefore, the other partners have the opportunity to express their interest in taking over these portfolios and to carry out the corresponding redistribution.

∴ No obligation to purchase lost portfolios

"No obligation in case of force majeure": In cases of force majeure the archiving library is not obliged to purchase again a potentially destroyed printed portfolio.

Responsibilities of the remaining cooperation partners:

The cooperation partners in general agree to hand over printed journal editions as whole or in part to the corresponding archiving libraries in case of need.

The remaining articles are typical contract terms such as confidentiality (Article 3), liability and force majeure (Article 4), term (Article 5), admission and suspension of cooperation partners (Article 6), law and jurisdiction (Article 7), and miscellaneous (Article 8).

Some topics such as the definition of due diligence were deliberately not elaborated in detail in the agreement as reaching a pragmatic and prompt agreement was a priority and a legal construction was chosen that allows the highest possible level of flexibility both in the implementation of the goals set and in the admission of new partners.

Content of the individual product agreement

Naming of the contracting parties

Article 1 Contractual framework conditions (= reference to the general cooperation agreement)

Article 2 Subject matter of the agreement
Subject matter of this agreement is the shared archiving of the printed journal editions of [*enter the name of the product*] according to Appendix 1.

Article 3 (In case of one) archiving library
The archiving library according to Article 2.4 of the general cooperation agreement for the portfolios as stated in this individual product agreement is [*enter the name of the library*].

Article 3 (In case of several) archiving libraries
Archiving libraries according to Article 2.4 of the general contract of cooperation for the portfolios as stated in this individual product agreement are laid down in Appendix 2.

Article 4 Transport
Transport of items has to be done in agreement between the delivering and archiving libraries, however at the latest by [*enter date*]. The contracting parties are obliged to carry out the transport of a portfolio with utmost care. Costs of transport are laid down in Appendix 2.

Article 5 Responsibilities and holdings records

The archiving library fulfils the responsibilities laid down in Article 2.5 of the general cooperation agreement by [*enter date*]. This deadline however does not apply to cataloguing and labelling of the portfolio as archived portfolio in the Austrian Union Catalogue; this has to be done 30 days after the handover of the respective printed journals at the latest.

Article 6 Information of cooperation partners

The contracting parties inform all other cooperation partners about the conclusion of this individual product agreement via email to the ubifo's secretariat.

Article 7 Entry into force

This individual product agreement enters into force with the signatures of all contracting parties.

All details concerning portfolios and handover regulations are documented in similar appendixes such as the following:

Appendix 2							
Title	**ISSN**	**Portfolio**	**Archiving library**	**Bestandsteile**	**Transfer**	**Transport costs**	**Comments**
Physical Review Series I and II	0031-899X	1.1893 - 35.1912 ; N.S. 1.1913 - 188.1969	UBW	1.1893 - 35.1912 ; N.S. 1.1913 - 188.1969	original portfolio UBW	–	
Physical Review A	0556-2791 ; 1050-2947	3.Ser. 1.1970 - 84.2011	UBW	1.1970 - 80.2009	original portfolio UBW	–	
				81.2010 - 84.2011	UBL to UBW	UBL	
Physical Review B	0556-2805 ; 0163-1829 ; 1098-0121	3.Ser. 1.1970 - 84.2011	UBW	1.1970 - 80.2009	original portfolio UBW	–	
				81.2010 - 84.2011	UBL to UBW	UBL	
Physical Review C	0556-2813	3.Ser. 1.1970 - 84.2011	UBW	1.1970 - 80.2009	original portfolio UBW	–	
				81.2010 - 84.2011	TUW to UBW	TUW	
Physical Review D	1550-7998 ; 0556-2821	3.Ser. 1.1970 - 84.2011	UBW	1.1970 - 80.2009	original portfolio UBW	–	
				81.2010 - 84.2011	TUW to UBW	TUW	
Physical Review E	1539-3755 ; 1063-651X	3.Ser. 47.1993 - 84.2011	UBW	1.1970 - 80.2009	original portfolio UBW	–	
				81.2010 - 84.2011	TUW to UBW	TUW	
Physical Review Letters	0031-9007	1.1958 - 107.2011	UBW	1.1958 - 103.2009	original portfolio UBW	–	
				104.2010 - 107.2011	UBL to UBW	UBL	
Reviews of Modern Physics	0034-6861	1.1929 - 83.2011	UBW	1.1929 - 81.2009	original portfolio UBW	–	
				82.2010 - 83.2011	TUW to UBW	TUW	

Figure 4.2: Appendix to individual product agreement.

On the basis of this legal structure and the defined workflows, archiving projects have been realised so far for the following products: American Physical Society (APS; 8 journals covering initially 46 holdings with 3.998 binding units were reduced to a best portfolio of 787 binding units) and Association for Computing Machinery (ACM; 144 journals[7]). In both cases the archived holdings were gathered in one library as this library already had a significant amount of printed holdings of this portfolio. However, this will or may not be the usual case in the future. Currently product agreements are under progress for the journals of the Institute of Physics (IOP) and the American Chemical Society (ACS).

Accompanying working infrastructure

Documenting the workload in the pilot project showed that appropriate communication and cooperation infrastructures have to be provided in order to be able to successfully continue shared archiving, as the work to coordinate libraries in shared archiving projects cannot be done in the long run without resources specifically dedicated to such projects. To this end a workspace in the form of a wiki was set up as networking tool for the contracting parties at the Austrian Library Network (Österreichische Bibliothekenverbund und Service GmbH, OBVSG)[8], which runs the Austrian Central Catalogue and the Austrian Search Interface. It was possible to implement this wiki fast and without additional administrative work due to the fact that all institutions participating in Shared Archiving Austria are members of the Austrian Library Network and as such their representatives were already authorised to work in the respective library systems by means of their user initials.

It was decided not to assign different authorisations for reading and writing in the wiki to the authorised wiki users as no sensitive data is stored in the wiki once the signature pages of the digitised contracts had been removed.

By setting up this accompanying infrastructure Shared Archiving Austria has been anchored at the centre of the three most important, cross-university library initiatives in Austria:

- the Council of Austrian University Libraries (ubifo) which bears the political will to support Shared Archiving Austria in order to reach common strategic goals by providing local library resources. Due to the fact that all ubifo libraries are in the same legal situation by being autonomous and by being part of state universities, archiving tasks can be fulfilled with the highest level of sustainability.

---

7 Counting of initial and archived binding units has not yet been completed.
8 Official website of OBVSG (https://www.obvsg.at/; last view on December 13th, 2017)

- the Austrian Academic Library Consortium (KEMÖ) as purchasing community for electronic licenses of which nearly all university libraries are members. Through the joint purchasing and licensing of electronic content the necessity of identical archival rights is given in many cases.
- the Austrian Library Network (OBVSG) which is in charge of managing nearly all existing metadata and user authorisations in the Austrian library landscape and which supplies various infrastructures for cross-library cooperation. Hence, it was possible to avoid expensive and training-intensive new administration tools.

Sections in the Shared Archiving wiki

General documents

This section is used to permanently document the general cooperation agreement, help texts, manuals and workflows in the library system, in the wiki and other resources and to save minutes of meetings, agendas and similar documents.

Contacts

This section includes contact persons in alphabetical order and by institutional affiliation as well as predefined mailing lists for different applications.

Archived products

This section shows product-specific individual agreements, lists of participants and contacts, titles lists and the status of the project.

Publications

This section covers lectures given and publications made in connection with the project, publications of other archiving initiatives and further literature (depending on the license, either saved as full text or provided as link).

Marketplace

The section marketplace provides a forum for all institutions to make suggestions for future archiving projects. This is done in a two-step procedure:

Step 1: The project initiator posts a suggestion for a new archiving project to all partner institutions including the product's name, a preliminary title list and a call for expression of interest within a specified short time period.

Step 2: In case of a critical mass of interested institutions, the partners agree on a person responsible for the product ("product manager") who organises the further proceeding. A detailed template on how to enter local holdings (titles

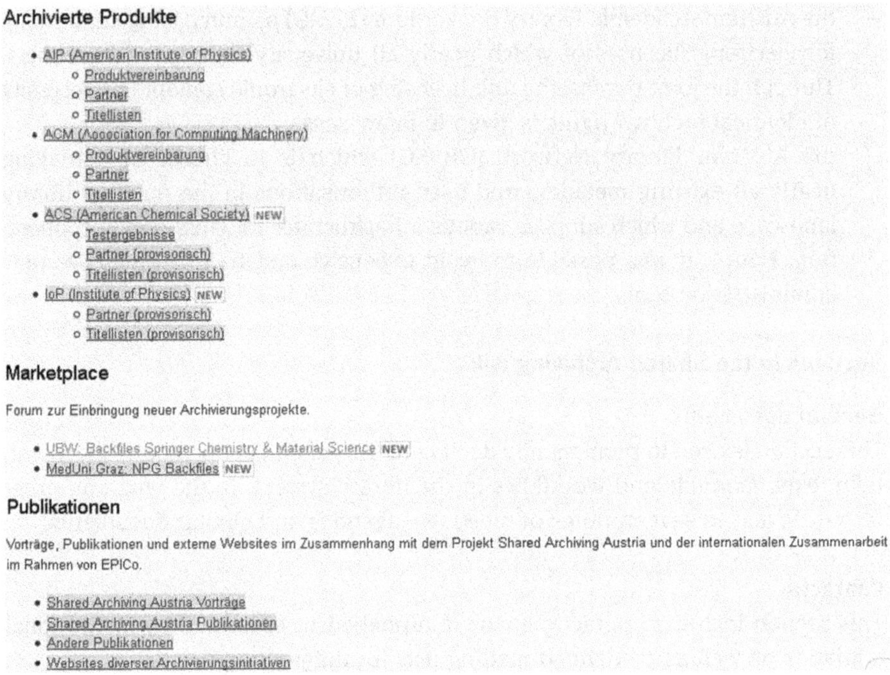

Archivierte Produkte

- AIP (American Institute of Physics)
  - Produktvereinbarung
  - Partner
  - Titellisten
- ACM (Association for Computing Machinery)
  - Produktvereinbarung
  - Partner
  - Titellisten
- ACS (American Chemical Society) NEW
  - Testergebnisse
  - Partner (provisorisch)
  - Titellisten (provisorisch)
- IoP (Institute of Physics) NEW
  - Partner (provisorisch)
  - Titellisten (provisorisch)

Marketplace

Forum zur Einbringung neuer Archivierungsprojekte.

- UBW: Backfiles Springer Chemistry & Material Science NEW
- MedUni Graz: NPG Backfiles NEW

Publikationen

Vorträge, Publikationen und externe Websites im Zusammenhang mit dem Projekt Shared Archiving Austria und der internationalen Zusammenarbeit im Rahmen von EPICo.

- Shared Archiving Austria Vorträge
- Shared Archiving Austria Publikationen
- Andere Publikationen
- Websites diverser Archivierungsinitiativen

Figure 4.3: Wiki – Marketplace (original German interface).

including title changes, supplements etc., the ISSN, ZDB numbers used in the periodicals database, AC system numbers generated in the Austrian Union Catalogue) is stored in the wiki.

The institutions make copies of the template, fill in the holdings information following a review of their holdings by autopsy (and add missing titles in case of need), enter their willingness to act as archiving library or as library handing over holdings and upload their copies as local information into the wiki.

The product manager combines the local holdings information in the template, pursues the project's progress and makes a proposal on how to distribute the printed holdings to suitable libraries based on what has been entered in the wiki and in consultation with the partners.

Due to the statements made by the partners on their willingness to either act as archiving library or hand over their holdings and the communication during the data collection, the decision on the distribution of the holdings to be archived can be taken quickly and efficiently.

The documents created during this work process can be used as appendixes for the future individual product agreement with only minor modifications being necessary.

Characteristics of Shared Archiving Austria

Finances:
- no central or other external funding;
- human resources are provided by the project partners;
- incurring costs (e.g. transport) are laid down in each individual product agreement and are taken over by the participating libraries.

Strengths:
- low costs;
- use of low-threshold, non-proprietary tools (MS Excel, wiki etc.); use of already existing technical resources;
- project anchored at the centre of the most important library initiatives in Austria (ubifo, KEMÖ and OBVSG);
- joint efforts, but also joint successes;
- sharpening of profiles of archiving libraries;
- improvement of standardised metadata and holdings.

Challenges:
- to motivate rectorates to reinvest the savings achieved by the reduction of floor space in libraries;
- the sustainability of the project depends on the opportunity and readiness of project partners to invest resources;
- project progress and pace depend also on free resources;
- the standardised display of holdings data has to be revised as there will be both ALMA and ALEPH libraries as of 2017/2018.

Excursus: International cooperation of archiving initiatives – EPICo

Official and private conversations led with representatives of other archiving initiatives in the frame of international conferences showed that despite of the various projects' differences there is a need for international exchange (going beyond conference lectures that cover the topics construction, collection management, strategy separately) and maybe also even for cooperation. As first step a panel discussion on collaborative storage was organised in the frame of an IFLA satellite meeting in Paris in 2014 together with Daryl Yang and Deborah Shorley, representing United Kingdom Research Reserve (UKRR). The results of this meeting were documented in two joint publications. Representatives from

Australia, New Zealand, Austria, France, the United Kingdom, the United States and Canada participated in this meeting.

The discussions following this meeting showed that focusing on European cooperation seemed more efficient due to legal, organisational and economic framework conditions. As a consequence, a first informal meeting of representatives of European archiving initiatives was held on November 19th 2015 at Vienna University Library. Participants were representatives of the Centre technique du livre de l'enseignement supérieur (CTLes, France), Garantia d'Espai per a la Preservació de l'Accés (GEPA, Catalonia), Kooperative Print-Archivierung (Switzerland), the National Repository Library Finland (Finland), the National Library of Norway (Norway), United Kingdom Research Reserve (UKRR) and Shared Archiving Austria.

At this meeting it was decided to cooperate and a mission statement was drafted:

"We believe that a comprehensive and robust research and information infrastructure is essential for Europe's wellbeing, now and in the future.

We are concerned that, at a time of unprecedented change in the ways information is collected, stored and disseminated, there is a real danger that some of the important printed resources in our European libraries may be at risk.

In view of this we intend to initiate a number of plans.[9]"

At a second meeting in Paris in May 2016 the name EPICo (European Print Initiatives Collaboration) was officially introduced and topics as well as corresponding actions plans were defined.

In order to be able to pursue these plans the following steps were taken:
- a common internal work space was set up;
- a questionnaire to register and catalogue European archiving initiatives was drawn up;
- a website showing printed holdings repositories worldwide (based on the preliminary work of Pentti Vattulainen, National Repository Library Finland)[10] was created and
- a model how to calculate savings from archiving activities was started.

In addition, the circle of members has been extended by Speicherverbund Nord, Bayerische Staatsbibliothek (both Germany) and the Estonian Repository Library (Estonia).

---

9 EPICo Website (http://www.varastokirjasto.fi/epico/; last view on December 13th, 2017)
10 Print Repositories Worldwide (http://www.varastokirjasto.fi/prw/; last view on December 13th, 2017)

References

Bauer, Bruno: *Austrian University Libraries on Their Way toward E-Only for Scholarly Journals.* Library Connect 9,1 (2011) p. 3.

DIN Deutsches Institut für Normung: *DIN-Fachbericht 13:2009-11. Bau- und Nutzungsplanung von Bibliotheken und Archiven.* Berlin 2009.

Kromp, Brigitte; Mayer, Wolfgang: *Gemeinsame Archivierung an den österreichischen Universitätsbibliotheken: Neues Geld statt altem Raum.* Universitätsbibliotheken im Fokus. Aufgaben und Perspektiven der Universitätsbibliotheken an öffentlichen Universitäten in Österreich (= Schriften der Vereinigung Österreichischer Bibliothekarinnen und Bibliothekare (VÖB) 13), ed. by Bruno Bauer. Graz 2013. p. 87–98 (http://hdl.handle.net/10760/24282).

Mouw, James: *Leaving the Collections Behind – Are we Ready?* Library Connect 9,1 (2011) p. 5.

Schmidt, Janine: *Panel Discussion on Collaborative Storage. A Global Perspective.* Space and Collections Earning their Keep (= IFLA Publications 175), ed. by Joseph Hafner; Diane Koen. Berlin, Boston 2016. p. 195–205.

Shorley, Deborah; Yang, Daryl; Kromp, Brigitte; Mayer, Wolfgang: *Collections Earning Their Keep. An Overview of International Archiving Initiatives.* 027.7 Zeitschrift für Bibliothekskultur 3,1 (2015) p. 30–46 (DOI: 10.12685/027.7-3-1-58).

Stieg, Kerstin; Pavlovic, Karlo: *Kooperative Lizenzierung von Online-Ressourcen in Österreich.* Mitteilungen der VÖB 63,3/4 (2010) p. 90–94.

Helen Renwick and Linda George

5 Outsourcing: a solution for New Zealand university libraries' print journals

Background

New Zealand is a small country in the Pacific with a population of 4.5 million. It has eight universities that range in size from 33,500 to 3,000 students and 5,000 to 680 staff.

The universities receive approximately 40% of their annual income from government grants. The remaining income is split evenly between student fees and other sources, principally research contracts and trading income. The representative body for the universities is Universities New Zealand – Te Pokai Tara (UNZ) and the eight vice-chancellors meet regularly.

The university librarians act collectively as the Council of New Zealand University Librarians (CONZUL) and report to UNZ. CONZUL's objective is to "improve access for students and staff of New Zealand universities to the information resources required to advance teaching, learning and research." In doing this, it "supports programmes that facilitate the sharing of knowledge, resources and enabling NZ university libraries to purchase resources collaboratively".[1]

The respective libraries' needs for storage to accommodate print collections has varied, depending on their histories. They ranged from larger libraries with relatively extensive collections that had outgrown their current accommodation and were urgently seeking more space, to considerably smaller libraries with no storage problems for the short term. Collaborative storage for low-use print collections had been on CONZUL's agenda for some time, despite the varying needs, and in 2009 a government grant enabled a librarian from a member library to be assigned to investigate international developments. The proposed concept was a purpose-built building, with environmental controls, for a print collection that was sorted by size, stowed in trays, given a fixed location and held indefinitely.[2]

---

1 Information about UNZ and CONZUL taken from http://www.universitiesnz.ac.nz/ 30 April 2017.

2 More background information on the history and development of the CONZUL Store can be found in *Helen Renwick, (2013), "Collaborative storage of print serials in New Zealand", Library Management*, Vol. 34 Iss 4/5 pp. 335–341.

https://doi.org/10.1515/9783110535372-005

However, in 2011 the University of Auckland commissioned a review of library storage options in relation to its own needs and shared the consultant's report with the other university librarians. Outsourcing to a commercial third party was one of several options presented for consideration and CONZUL was quick to decide that it would be adequate for the storage of print journals.

Later that same year, a contract was agreed between a document management company and UNZ and what is referred to as the CONZUL Store came into existence.

The contract is for storage until 2023 when both the contract and the need to retain the print journals for a further period will be reviewed.

Outsourcing was not seen as a complete answer to the university libraries' need for storage. It was an expedient and pragmatic solution for large collections that had been superseded by e-journals, which would ease the pressure on collection accommodation.

The CONZUL Store

The primary objectives of the CONZUL Store[3] project were to:
- Preserve a copy of print serial publications for the New Zealand research communities and
- Rationalise serial collection holdings and utilize library accommodation efficiently.

In recommending to UNZ that print serials be consigned to commercial storage, CONZUL had in mind primarily those titles that are produced by the large publishing companies and that are also available on secure platforms as e-journals. The New Zealand university libraries had been early adopters of e-journals with an expressed preference for electronic only subscriptions, ie specifically they did not want to continue acquiring print copies as well. This position raised the question of the value of storing the print versions at all. Why retain old print copies when publishers' licences provided access to digitized versions and the libraries were deliberately choosing the electronic format?

Although LOCKSS and Portico had been established a few years previously, there was discussion among librarians at the time about the number of print

---

3 "CONZUL Store" refers to the shared collection, distributed among several locations, while "store" or "storage facility" generally means one of the commercial provider's buildings.

copies that should be retained worldwide to ensure preservation. In that context, New Zealand might have been seen as a relatively safe place for a depository. At a national level, the tertiary education sector had been operating in a competitive environment for some time and the government was keen to foster more collaboration among the universities. Cooperating in the storage of a shared collection was one project that could demonstrate that the universities were working together. There was still some unease among academic staff about the electronic format, and retrospectively digitized journals were sometimes found to be imperfect. Librarians and vice-chancellors were both aware of the risk of negative publicity arising from the disposal of what had been a considerable financial investment in scholarly journals.

On balance, it was decided that a single shared copy of each print serial should be retained. All the libraries agreed to participate and share the costs, even though some of them had no current need for storage and not all were persuaded of the need to retain print journals when they had access to electronic versions.

The storage options

The building consultant who carried out the review for the University of Auckland Library presented ten storage options. They were variations of new build or building conversion, plus outsourcing. The main variables for all options were environmental controls and building size.

The new build options involved building a new store on university-owned land or leasing a commissioned building from a developer, both on and off campus.

The other options involved the conversion of an existing building to serve as a library store. The building could have been one owned by a university or leased from another party.

In all the cases that involved new building or converting an existing building, it was envisaged that the material would be stored in cartons with a fixed shelf location, following the examples of the Harvard Depository[4] and CAVAL's CARM Centre[5]. The building might have been single storey (low stud) or double height (medium stud) with a mesh floor between the stacks, again like the CARM store.

---

4 http://hul.harvard.edu/hd/
5 http://www.caval.edu.au/carm.html

Table 5.1: Storage options and financial impacts.

	Option	Description	Financial Impact			Overall qualitative impact
			Capital required Year 1	Cost in nominal terms p.a.	NPV cost	
1	New university building, off campus	2,325 m² Purpose-built, low stud with environmental control	33.6	3.2	2.9	Excellent
2	New developer led building, off campus, leased	2,325 m² Purpose-built, low stud with environmental control	5.1	4.1	3.7	Excellent
3	New university building, on campus	2,.25 m² Purpose-built, low stud with environmental control	27.6	2.8	2.7	Excellent
4	New university building, off campus	1,675 m² Purpose-built, medium stud, with no environmental control	26.6	2.5	2.3	Moderate
5	Building conversion, leased	2,.72 m² Conversion of existing building, with environmental control	4.9	2.8	2.6	Good
6	Building conversion, leased	2,572 m² Conversion of existing building, with no environmental control	4.9	2.3	2.2	Moderate
7	Building conversion, university owned	2,572 m² Conversion of existing building, with environmental control	22.4	2.6	2.4	Good
8	Building conversion, university owned	2,572 m² Conversion of existing building, no environmental control	20.3	2.2	2.0	Moderate
9	Outsourced, off campus	75,000 cartons, no environmental control	1	1	1	Moderate
10	Outsourced, off campus	75,000 cartons, with environmental control	1	1.9	1.9	Excellent

The ten storage options were evaluated in terms of financial impact and overall quality. The financial measures were the capital required in the first year, nominal costs per annum, and net present value costs (NPV). The overall quality of each option was assessed as excellent, good or moderate.

All the storage options with environmental control rated higher on "overall qualitative impact" than the options without. They were also considerably more expensive, for obvious reasons. For instance, the NPV cost of outsourced storage with environmental storage is almost twice that of outsourced storage without such controls.

The building options, whether new build or conversion, all required considerable capital upfront. A "new build, off campus" store would have required almost 34 times more capital in the first year than either of the outsourced options. "New build, on campus" was also high in terms of first year capital requirements, while leasing buildings was much lower.

Outsourcing would not provide purpose-built accommodation with the assurance of permanent retention but it clearly had financial factors in its favour. It was relatively inexpensive and did not need a large capital investment. Funding could come from operational budgets and there would be no long lead-time for planning and building processes. It was pragmatic and expedient, it would provide relief for overcrowded collections and it was achievable immediately.

The options are compared in Table 5.1, where actual costs, now outdated, have been substituted by ratios. The value of each financial measure of the selected option (outsourcing without environmental controls) has been set at one.

The current situation

CONZUL was not constituted in a way that allowed it to enter into a legal commitment with the storage company so UNZ became the contract partner. The print journals have been depreciated and are gifted to UNZ. They are to be in good condition and bound volumes are preferred, for convenience.

The storage company's facilities are distributed across both islands of New Zealand, as are participating universities. Journal volumes are packed in closed cartons and stored, without environmental control, in any one of the several stores operated by the company across the country, but usually in the facility nearest the depositing library. The collection is therefore held in several locations.

The North and South Islands are separated by Cook Strait and served by both frequent ferry and airfreight services, so the geographical distribution of material is not detrimental to the fulfilment of requests, which are predominantly for scanned single articles.

The material is not generally available for circulation, so each storage facility has a reading room for the use of researchers who wish to consult the collection, and the company makes a scanner and a fax machine available. The service requirements and quality standards include a regular programme of pest management, cleaning and building maintenance, checking for mould, and monitoring of temperature and humidity levels.

The choice to deposit, or not, is contingent on each library's situation: the extent and age of their serial collections, duplication with online equivalents and print only holdings, their own capacity for accommodating and retaining print, and cost-effectiveness.

Strategic decisions regarding rationalisation of collections and re-purposing of library spaces may be drivers for lodgement in the Store, or exceptional circumstances such as the Canterbury earthquakes in 2011 when the University of Canterbury had need for alternative space at short notice. Those with small print collections, whose core subjects and more recent collection development result in predominantly online serials, have no need to deposit. Other libraries have adequate accommodation at present. Annual deposits are variable on account of these factors.

To date six of the eight member libraries have deposited material into the shared Store.

There are now more than 236,000 volumes in the CONZUL Store. (There were already 3,506 volumes in the company's stores under pre-existing contracts with individual libraries and these were incorporated.) This represents an increase of approximately 63% since the Store was established.

Table 5.2: Volumes lodged each year.

2012	2013	2014	2015	2016	2017*[6]	Total
158, 375	40,729	11,508	5,056	14,755	2,270	232,693

Bibliographic access to the stored collection is provided via the catalogue of the donor university library and via the National Bibliographic Database hosted by National Library of New Zealand.

There are two other sites for identifying material that is held in the shared Store but neither functions as a library catalogue. One is a spreadsheet of titles and their holdings that is hosted by UNZ and the other is the company's database.

---

6 As at April 2017

UNZ provides a purpose built extranet for CONZUL member libraries to record information about the Store. Designated staff from each library have access to the extranet and the supporting documentation, which includes policy statements, procedural manuals relating to lodgement processes, and other relevant information.

There is a calendar to register lodgement dates so that only one library is making a deposit at any time, which is a requirement if duplication is to be avoided. There is also a spreadsheet that summarises, by way of titles and associated holdings, all the material that is held in storage and available on request to the university libraries. Details of all items delivered to the storage company at its various locations around New Zealand are uploaded to this spreadsheet.

The storage company provides a template for uploading information to its database. Essentially, this comprises journal titles plus item and carton barcodes, for the purpose of facilitating retrieval from its stores. The database has more information about the collection than the UNZ spreadsheet but it too has limited search capabilities.

Each title is distinguished as being in one of two categories when it is lodged: there are those that are available on a secure electronic platform under a permanent licence, and the rest that are a minority that are print only and some others for which perpetual access is not assured. This information is intended to facilitate an assessment of the collection the contract comes to its end. The bulk of titles fall into the first category.

Requests for material from the store have been made almost exclusively by one library. There have not been many and overall they are in decline. A proportion of requests is received from non-member libraries through inter-library loan, and the standard applicable fee for this service is charged to the requesting library.

Reasons for patron requests are usually associated with omissions from, or the poor quality of, available online equivalents. Requests are also made by library staff to fulfil course reading requirements and comply with copyright.

Table 5.3: Requests for articles from CONZUL Store.

2012	2013	2014	2015	2016	2017[7]	Total
38	289	174	115	114	27	730

A library that chooses to contribute material to the Store carries the costs of identifying the titles it will offer and of checking them against the UNZ

---

7 As at April 2017

spreadsheet to ensure there is no duplication with material that has already been deposited.

It also has the costs of selecting and packing the volumes, arranging transport with the company, and preparing spreadsheets of titles and barcodes for uploading to both UNZ's spreadsheet and the company's database.

These can be construed as "hidden costs", inherent in the preliminary process of lodgement. They vary among libraries, depending on the availability of human and physical resources.

The costs of cartons, which are supplied by the company for holding the journal volumes, and of the monthly storage are shared. These costs are allocated among the member libraries on the basis of an equal share of a fixed portion and the remainder in proportion to the amount of funding that each university receives from government. The company invoices the libraries individually on a monthly basis for their share of the storage plus any retrieval costs that they may have incurred.

Assessment by stakeholders

UNZ and CONZUL were asked to comment on whether the storage project was meeting its objectives, specifically:
- To rationalize the retention of low-use print research collections
- To release library building space
- To moderate the costs of further library buildings
- To preserve print research collections
- To provide effective access to stored research collections

Responses indicate that the CONZUL Store is generally regarded as successful.

One university librarian wrote that "The principle of a shared store of last copy ... has been a very efficient way to address a problem ... rather than all libraries duplicating holdings", although another noted that "This hasn't been a lot of assistance to us as we have discarded most of the journals to which we have electronic access ... I don't believe that we have discarded any print material because it is in the CONZUL Store, but have only done so when we have secured ongoing electronic access."

Seven of the eight libraries replied that the CONZUL Store had released library space. "It has released considerable library building space and allowed us to both create new study spaces and move our information commons ... The ability to change library space is increasingly a very valuable benefit of a shared service." "Changes to the use of library building space and the fact that electronic versions of serials are more prolific, stable and accepted by users and library staff means that destruction of hard copy versions of perpetually held serials is a safe option." One library, with a good deal of its serials already in storage, replied that "We would gain greater release of space if we were able to lodge books because our periodicals are shelved separately and in [compact moveable shelving], thus our space issues are primarily caused by books on other floors."

The shared store appears to have mitigated the demand for further library building: "The Store has acted as a cost-effective and useful collection 'parking space' while decisions are made locally on individual members' library buildings and collections", "Access to print volumes was maintained without expenditure on shelving and buildings" and "The reduction in footprint taken up by print serials has been an important element in the development of a business case to transform the library building from a storehouse of collections to space for people, learning and community. While we still do require a new storage facility (outside the current library) for low use books, the size required is considerably reduced due to the ability to discard or move serials to the shared store."

There was less confidence that the Store was meeting its preservation objective. Five years after its establishment, some members expressed doubts about the need to retain print journals at all, where there is a secure and perpetual electronic version. One reflected that view in saying "Agreement should been reached on some JSTOR titles to be excluded from the CONZUL Store". The other members made no comment.

In terms of access, one library regretted the inability to walk in and browse but otherwise found that its single requesting experience had been "easy and the article arrived quickly". Another said that "It was good to outsource to a provider with bases across the country" and "Items can be out of sequence and it doesn't matter". The library that has been the most frequent user wrote that "Patrons from all levels make requests for material and some inter-loan requests are fulfilled."

Conclusion

CONZUL has outsourced storage of print journals to a commercial supplier that has facilities across the country. The arrangement was not seen as a full answer to the need for storage of the universities' print collections but rather as an opportunity to address an immediate problem. The journals are being held until 2023 and the need to retain them longer will be reassessed in another five years' time. In the meantime, stakeholders are generally satisfied that by sharing a single copy they have collaborated for efficiency and preserved a large print research collection, just in case.

Ulrich Niederer

6 Supporting libraries: Setting up the Cooperative Storage Library Switzerland

Introduction

The Cooperative Storage Library Switzerland (CSLS) has, after a long planning period, been operational since Feb. 2016. In this book, there are two papers by this author and by Christian Oesterheld (in the following chapter). Each covers different aspects of the same project. The two authors present the thinking behind the CSLS and its daily operation, aiming both at making storage safe and economic for libraries and guaranteeing users easy access. They discuss setting up cooperation, economic and political aspects, technology used, as well as storage principles (in relation to use), de-duplicating some of the material stored, building a shared repository of print journals and questions as to the ease of use. They are candid about the difficulties and the discussions that are going on, e.g. users find it difficult to get used to the idea that 'their' material is held off-site; that e-coverage of relevant serial titles, notably in the HSS disciplines, is not as full as was expected; or that the serials in the shared journal repository of the CSLS are only available via article copies and cannot be browsed anymore on site. The conclusion gives a personal, balanced but open view as to where the CSLS is successful and what needs perfecting, and points out some of the strategies currently developed to enhance the usefulness of the CSLS both for libraries and users.

Pre-history: an idea

In 1993, Hubert Villard, former director of the *Bibliothèque Cantonale et Universitaire* in Lausanne, started his seminal essay[1] with a few interesting remarks about the development of library holdings. He includes the well-known observation of their exponential growth: a library's holdings usually double each generation, or in alternative numbers: each century since Gutenberg's invention has

---

1 Villard, Hubert (1993). "Du bassin d'accumulation au réservoir d'eau vive : vers une gestion dynamique des collections", in *L'espace bibliothéconomique Suisse : hier, aujourd'hui, demain. En hommage à Gustave Moeckli*, edited by Gabrielle von Roten and Martin Nicoulin (Vevey: Edition de l'Aire). pp 343–362.

https://doi.org/10.1515/9783110535372-006

seen a proven six fold growth. How to cope with this growth? Villard reminds his readers of the fact that US libraries built more new space in the decade from 1965 to 1975 than ever before, space for storage for up to an additional 163 mio volumes. But in the same period, these libraries showed a growth of 166 mio volumes … Thus, simply adding space cannot provide a long term solution.

Hubert Villard goes on to develop the idea of library and storage as a series of interdependent facilities: from open access areas with the latest and most heavily used material to on-site storage which in turn is backed up by off-site storage. An off-site storage facility could offer cooperative services to a number of libraries, like de-duplicating lesser used material.

In 1994, the author of this article, Ulrich Niederer, went on a study tour in the US that led to several cooperative storage facilities, among them the Medical Library Center in New York, the Harvard Depository in Boston, the Center for Research Libraries in Chicago, and the Southern Regional Library Facility of the University of California at Los Angeles. The principal insights, much abbreviated, were that cooperation allows for de-duplication and substantial space savings, and that cooperation also furthers the development of services above and beyond mere storage and delivery. In fact, the institutions which were particularly successful in offering innovative services on top of storage – added value, you could call it – were also those that developed from basic storage facilities into broader and very lively library service centers.

Upon his report to one of Switzerland's library associations a working group was established. Its primary aim was to find out more about the economic basics for such a scheme in Switzerland, and whether there was enough actual interest to start planning a cooperative storage facility. Hubert Villard and Ulrich Niederer as well as representatives from five other major Swiss libraries were part of this working group. – To cut an interesting story short: the working group was only partly successful: it succeeded in identifying an interest of Swiss libraries in the idea. But the interest proved to be theoretical in that most participating libraries judged the concept to be highly interesting but that they themselves did not have an actual need for storage capacity and therefore saw no possibility to participate in planning. Furthermore the group did not succeed to commission an economic study to show beyond doubts the advantages of a shared storage facility. It went, to put it succinctly, to sleep.

History: an evaluation

But it turned out to be a fitful sleep, in which dreams of storage cooperation lived on. In 2005, the Lucerne Central and University Library started to evaluate an off-site storage facility for its own needs. Cooperation lurked in the wings, but at first it was strictly about storing the holdings of the Lucerne library with enough reserve room to possibly make further planning unnecessary.

The evaluation had a vision: to find the best possible solution for an off-site storage facility – best in terms of economics as well as preservation. An off-site situation was a given, as it was clear that there was no possibility to store present and future holdings in the middle of the city, a city that is plagued by high real estate costs as well as by a high water table that does not easily allow for multi-storey underground constructions. The evaluation team was led by a member of the cantonal Office of Buildings and Construction (Jörg Enzmann, principal project manager), had three members of the library (Ulrich Niederer, director, Katharina Mettler, head of preservation/conservation, Philipp Marti, head IT), and it contracted the support of an external logistics consultant (Jürgen Rammerstorfer, Ralog Engineering). The evaluation method consisted in a detailed comparison of various storage models: fixed shelving, movable shelving, high bay construction with manual service ("Harvard type"), and auto-mated high bay (automated storage and retrieval system, ASRS) that included preservation factors, ergonomics factors, and economic factors. These last eco-nomic factors included a full cost analysis of all models (with capital costs, maintenance costs, and operation costs), resulting in a figure for costs per volume per year.

The evaluation was based on a set of given factors for comparison: size (1.5 mio volumes, with a possibility of extension), preservation (18° Celsius, +/– 2°; 45% rel. humidity, +/– 5%), and delivery (wait 1 full day max, Mon to Sat). The evaluation also developed all models in a very detailed and concrete way so as to be able to determine realistic and comprehensive reports on cost, but also on preservation and ergonomic factors.

The evaluation soon identified four central cost factors:
- real estate costs (tied to the surface needed by a storage model)
- wages and labour regulations
- fire prevention
- steel cost

The first two factors are determined locally, they may differ from one region or country to the next. In Switzerland, real estate costs are high – we are therefore interested in a small "footprint". Comparing the four storage models led to the following results.

Labour regulations determine the kind of employee you can (or have to) hire, and accordingly his or her wages. If you are bound by regulations to hire professionals, eg for driving order pickers in Harvard type storage facilities, your wages are going to be higher than if you can hire students for the same job.

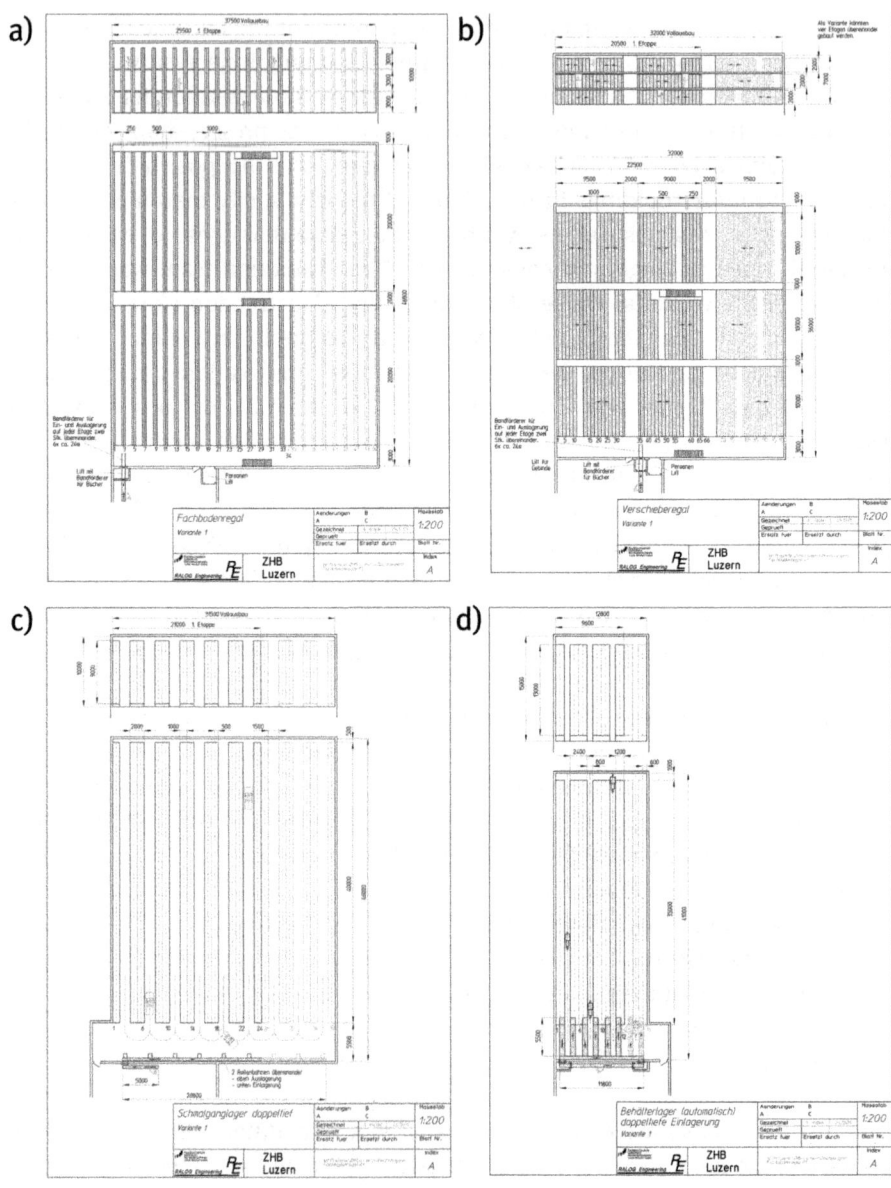

Figure 1: Layout plans for the surface of different storage systems.
Comparison factors:
a) Fixed shelving: 1, b) Movable shelving: 0.68, c) Harvard type: 0.85, d) ASRS: 0.32
© for all plans: Ralog AG Zofingen (Switzerland)

The third and fourth factors are probably very general ones and fairly immune to local or regional influences. Fire prevention in a storage area will be achieved most commonly by sprinklers, by an infusion of a fire suppressing gas, if allowed, or by constant oxygen reduction. In an area in which people are working, sprinkler systems are probably most common, gas is difficult because of the number of emergency exits you have to provide, and constant oxygen reduction is not possible. An automated area in which no people work regularly could make use of oxygen reduction. Sprinklers would be more complex and hence costly, both for installation and for maintenance, especially in high bay constructions.

Steel cost is determined by the general construction: a high bay construction needs more steel but no floors. But more importantly: are shelves needed or not? Fixed or mobile shelving and Harvard type high bays do need shelves, an automated high bay construction needs angles of steel on which to place the containers. If calculated for 1.5 mio volumes, the savings in steel that can be realized by using angles instead of shelves come up to 7'000 m2!

Incidentally, the type of container used is probably also an interesting cost factor: some automated library storage facilities use steel containers (e.g. Mary Idema Pew Library and Steelcase Library of the Grand Valley State University in Allendale and Grand Rapids, MI (USA), the Joe and Rika Mansueto Library of the University of Chicago or the National Library of Norway in Mo i Rana). The Lucerne project uses plastic containers (standard sized, 60 × 40 cm), as does the Additional Storage Building of the British Library in Boston Spa (100 × 40 or 60 cm); both use emission-free plastic. Harvard-type storage facilities typically use cardboard trays (of varying width and height, but usually 45 cm long). However, we have no knowledge of any detailed cost comparison.

When these findings were combined, the result pointed clearly to an automated high bay storage facility: the order of the four models were: Harvard type (place 4), mobile shelving (place 3), fixed shelving (place 2), and ASRS (place 1). The 'cost per volume per year'-figure for the last two models were roughly $1.05 for fixed shelving, and $0.89 for the ASRS. When all the factors were taken into account, i.e. preservation, ergonomics, economics, the result was the same: the ASRS reached a top mark of 100%, whereas fixed shelving came to 91% only.

At that point, our funding body, the government of the Canton of Lucerne, asked for a comparison of the ASRS model to an outsourcing model: all holdings are entrusted to a logistics enterprise which stores them according to our preservation conditions. It also fulfils orders and delivers all documents to the library. This idea held a lot of appeal for our government, for two reasons: it corresponds to a more general tendency of a lean economy, and it promised

Figure 2: Fire prevention system. (top) Nitrogen plant in the CSLS, (bottom) Gas tanks (Inergen) and distribution control at the National Library of Austria.

Figure 2a: Sprinklers and fire prevention in high bay storage facilities. Both pictures show fire prevention installations in Yale's Harvard type Library Shelving Facility (as seen on a visit in 2004)

not to generate any investment (i.e. construction) costs. The library was more sceptical, for several reasons: an off-site storage solution has to offer a safe and stable long-term perspective – and what is 'long-term' in the fast-moving world of private enterprise? It also seemed quite difficult to react to a breach of conditions: if, e.g., preservation conditions were violated repeatedly so that the contract would have to be cancelled, how easy would it be to find a new storage facility and to move all holdings within a reasonable time? The library also argued that storage was one of the core competences of libraries, something which they had practiced and refined for centuries; outsourcing usually aims at peripheral activities, not at core competencies. And finally, the library director used his international contacts to single out other examples of outsourcing. In 2007, he found just one example: the Royal Library of Denmark ran a trial for ca. 150'000 volumes (or 5'000 linear metres) of litte use material. When it became clear that the first – optimistic and political – price offers of ca. $1 per order were too low and had to be raised to a maximum of $2, the trial turned into a provisional solution until construction for a new library storage facility was completed.

Figure 3: High bay storage types – shelves and steel angles. (top) Steel angles in the CSLS (bottom) Shelves in the CTLes, Paris. Photograph by Katharina Mettler.

Figure 4: Types of containers.
a) Harvard type (Yale Library Shelving Facility: cardboard, 45 cm long, varying width and height)
b) ASRS (CSLS: plastic, 60 cm x 40 cm, two heights: 25 cm and 35 cm)

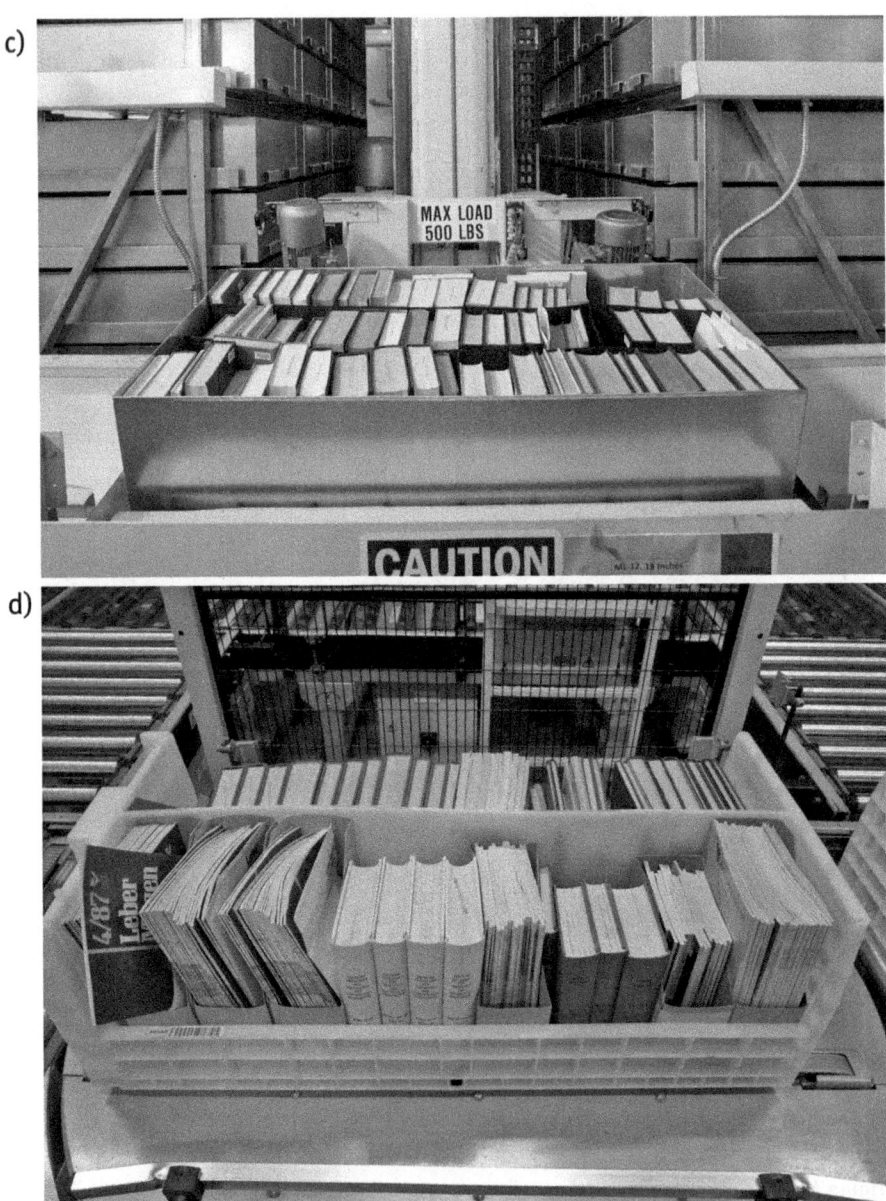

Figure 4: (continued)
c) ASRS (Mansueto Library, University of Chicago, ASR facility: steel, 48 x 24 inches /
121.92 x 60.96 cm, three heights: 10, 12 or 15 inches / 25.40 cm, 30.48 cm, 38.10 cm)
d) ASRS (British Library, Boston Spa: plastic, 100 cm x 60 or 40 cm, one height)

Nevertheless: to arrive at a "politically correct" comparison, we had to go through a formal GATT/WTO tender procedure. Three firms offered their services; the best offer equalled the costs of the ASRS solution, $0.89 per volume per year. Of course the major difference was in the relation between investment and running costs: while the outsourcing solution had very low investment and high running costs, it was the other way round with an ASRS built by the library resp. its funding body: high investment for construction, but comparatively low running and operating costs.

Cooperation – from possibility to reality

The outsourcing tender procedure was held in summer 2007. At the same time the working group started looking at the possibility of other libraries being open to sharing a storage facility. The background to this was a first enquiry into the cost effect of enlarging the building. It was found that a building for 3 mio volumes (i.e. double the size of the original evaluation) would lower costs per volume per year from $0.89 to $0.78, a building for three times the volumes, i.e. for 4.5 mio volumes, would bring the overall costs down to $0.71. The director of the Lucerne Central and University Library presented the evaluation and its findings at the regular meetings of the Swiss university and research libraries and the Swiss cantonal libraries; within a short time he found seven institutions who had not only an interest in cooperating but also an acute need to find new storage space. After it was established that cooperation was a realistic possibility they wrote to the government of the Canton of Lucerne stating explicitly that a) each institution was prepared to cooperate in planning, setting up und running a shared storage facility, and that b) each institution would participate only in a project fully owned and operated by the libraries (or their funding bodies); an outsourcing project was not an option for any of the interested institutions.

On this basis, the Lucerne government stopped the outsourcing tender, closed the evaluation formally, accepted the leading role in the new intercantonal working group to plan and prepare the realization of a cooperative storage facility, and delegated two Lucerne members, one of them the library director, to participate. Work started in 2009; quite quickly, it became evident that the most difficult job was to find a political framework to guarantee a generally acceptable governance structure.

There are two reasons for that: Switzerland has a rather weak central, i.e. federal structure and a very strong decentralised, federalist structure of 26 cantons. Culture and education up to the university level are the responsibility of the cantons. The federal state may pay subsidies and try and establish nation-wide standards, but most decisions are in the power of the cantons. The second reason is the fact that no canton wanted to invest preliminarily and then rent parts of the facility to the other cantons. On the contrary: The governing bodies of the participating libraries stipulated explicitly that the storage library had to be set up as an independent institution, not as an affiliate of one of the libraries that other libraries could use, and also that the storage library was to be financially independent, i.e. it would have to recover all its costs, capital (or rent), maintenance, operations etc.

This political part of the planning process took a good four years of intensive work, from 2009 to the end of 2013. The solution that was found led to separating ownership of the building from its operations. Ownership – and construction – of the building became the task of a stock corporation or public limited corporation; its shares are held by interested funding bodies (not all funding bodies were interested), and it had to acquire the financial means necessary for construction on the money market as mortgages. The plc rents the building to the association that the participating libraries form; this association is responsible for all operational matters, including hiring the CEO of the storage library who in turn hires all the other personnel. It is also responsible for developing and pursuing a strategy and for finding new members, i.e. new participating libraries. Being able to integrate new libraries has been a core point from the beginning, and the structure and bylaws of both the plc and the association allow for easy extension!

In fact, one new library has already joined the CSLS since it started its operations in February 2016, bringing up the library total to six (of the original eight libraries that formed the first working group, three had to drop out for various reasons: severe budget cuts, change in the principal library strategy of one canton, change in legal status from independent institution to being integrated into a bigger institution); the five founding libraries are the Library of the University of Basel (UB BS), the Central and University Library of Luzern (ZHB LU), the Central Library of Solothurn (ZB SO), the Central Library of Zurich (ZB ZH), and the Libraries of the University of Zurich (B UZH). The sixth member joining in late summer 2017 is the Library of the University of St. Gallen (UB SG).

Principles of technical services

Soon after the principal working group started to work on political and legal matters, a second group was set up for all aspects of operations: the Operations Working Group. It defined the basic principles and routines, e.g.:

- the CSLS is a library for libraries; users do not interact with the CSLS directly;
- in fact, users should not need to know that there is a CSLS. For them, the CSLS is like any other (off-site) storage site of their library, and an order from the holdings of their library is fulfilled regardless of where that particular item is stored;
- this means that there should be a fully integrated interface between the library management systems and the warehouse management system of the CSLS.

Services should be of the best possible quality. From the beginning they would include the following:
- document delivery in physical or electronic form should be a standard service;
- physical delivery is mainly monographs. The majority of these were expected to go to the libraries where users would fetch them. Physical deliveries would use a courier service; integration with the already existing courier service would be the preferred solution;
- physical delivery could go to a home address of an end user vial postal service;
- electronic delivery of journal articles should go directly to the end-user;
- if a user wants to consult a whole journal run, he or she could use the small reading room at the CSLS; appointments to be made via the user's home library;
- service to users of the participating libraries is a priority, but service to the libraries themselves is of equal importance;
- further services can and should be developed – in fact, this will be an essential driver for the healthy development of the CSLS itself.

The Operations Working Group also defined the two pre-conditions for libraries to become part of the CSLS: every item must be catalogued and have a barcode. This ensures proper communication between the library management system (LMS) and the warehouse management system (WMS). An 'item' typically is a monograph or a journal volume; it is important that journal volumes are itemised explicitly in the catalogue (and not just mentioned summarily under 'holdings') to guarantee easy and safe ordering of articles. But sometimes items are stored in (collective) boxes; it is possible to give the box a barcode and order the whole box. It would even be possible to give a barcode only to a whole container; the 'item' thus would be the whole container, and ordering this item would bring all the contents of the container. This could be an interesting option for uncatalogued material that is awaiting cataloguing (but probably not an option for material not intended for cataloguing).

The other pre-condition is: every item is cleaned, i.e. its exterior is thoroughly de-dusted. The intertior of an item is not examined in the CSLS; it is the responsibility of each library not to deliver contaminated material! 'Item' here means 'physical item'; thus, item in boxes have to be cleaned, too. Libraries can de-dust their holdings themselves, shortly before delivering them to the CSLS. Or they can ask the CSLS to do it for them; the CSLS is equipped with book-cleaning machines and will charge libraries for this service.

Perhaps the most important and certainly the most public topic the Operations Working Group had to treat was the de-duplication project. The earliest ideas included the de-duplication of journal holdings; titles which occur in two or more libraries could be checked for completeness and quality of state; the best copy would be kept in collective ownership, and the libraries owning redundant copies would be free to do with them as they pleased: discard them, keep them, sell them... After several tests the overlap potential was estimated to be at around 30%; with over a million journal volumes intended for the new collective holdings, savings would thus be at around 300'000 volumes or 10 linear km! It is not astonishing that such figures furnished one of the most powerful arguments in favour of a shared, cooperative storage, especially for funding bodies and politicians involved.

But as tempting as these figures are, the project caused considerable work in all libraries. The five founding libraries looked for a way to determine the best copy, and they commissioned a custom software from a library consulting firm (Trialog, Switzerland) that allowed the import of the title and holdings data of journals from the library catalogues, determined the best copy, taking into consideration that the two biggest libraries were designated as default libraries for their respective subjects, and identified missing blocks (if indicated in the original data). It also proposed the best copy, and it allowed to alter the proposals online and in real time during the checking the library personnel had to do in the stacks. In short: It worked, even if it was hard and long work – developing and testing the software took the better part of a year, and the actual work, determining and checking the copies for the collective holdings took another year and a half.

Other topics turned out to be more straightforward, like defining the courier and finding an integrative solution with the existing courier service (see below, p. 78), or finding a solution for an integrated scanning process that allowed a partial automation of an order from a library up to sending off the scan to the user and billing facts to the library which sends the bill to the user. Here we were again lucky in that we could build on a solution from a German firm, Imageware, that was already in use in three of the five libraries.

At the core of all operations is of course the interface between the library management systems and the warehouse management system. Even if – by

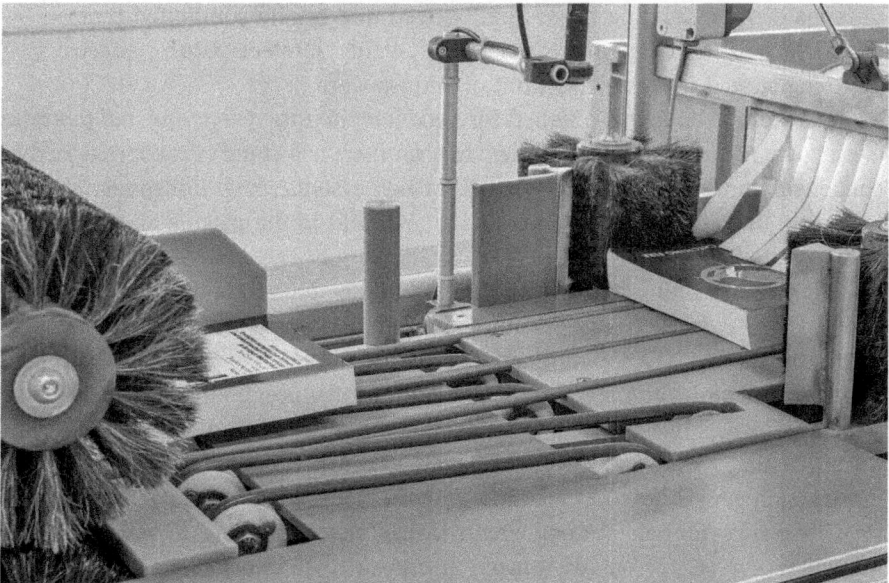

Figure 5: (top) Book cleaning machine, (bottom) Detail of the cleaning process. Photograph by Mike Märki

chance, not by design or exclusion – all participating libraries use Ex Libris' Aleph 500 and belong to the Information Network of the University Libraries of German speaking Switzerland (Informationsverbund Deutschschweiz, IDS) as members or partners, it was necessary to set up individual interfaces between each LMS and the WMS. This also proved to be a details-rich task of no trivial scope

When setting up the principal Operations Working Group or sub-groups for specific tasks, it was very important to have librarians from all participating libraries in the groups. This might seem like overkill – after all, these people put in a lot of hours. But we realized that these topics were not only technical questions, but also great possibilities to build understanding for the differences of the libraries going to work together, and to create trust! Trust, we learned, cannot be overestimated in a multi-partner project.

Construction: maximum density, minimal footprint, as sustainable as possible

After all political questions had found an answer acceptable to everyone, and all libraries or their funding bodies had agreed and finally committed themselves definitively to the cooperative project – towards summer 2014 –, construction planning started in earnest. Central principles were:

The storage area was planned for *maximum density with a minimal footprint* (see above, Figure 1). It has six aisles, in each there is a crane or robot that fetches containers and brings them to a conveyor belt system which transports the container out of the oxygen reduced storage area and to the picking stations in the administrative area.

High bay facilities enable by definition highly dense storage; compared to a Harvard type storage facility the automated storage profits from larger containers and narrower aisles. And while automation for storage has become an accepted industry standard, the CSLS introduced one new feature: its robots use two load handling devices but place them one above the other instead side by side. Thus the aisles are 84 cm wide instead of at least 150 cm – this gave us one whole aisle more which equals 500'000 volumes without changing the surface layout.

The conveyor belt system which brings the containers to and from the administrative area is usually placed at one side of the aisles. In order to save that surface area for shelving, we placed it above the shelving and in the middle of the storage building, with two advantages: we could use the whole storage area surface for shelving, and we could stick with a standard height of shelving

Figure 6: Robot (part) with two load-handling devices, one above the other

and with standard cranes: standards are cost effective. Finally, the shelving construction was planned so as to survive minor to middle earthquakes with very little or no damage to the goods stored.

Modularity was a central part in the project, from its earliest beginnings. It has two aims: one is of course to be able to add further storage units as new libraries want to join, the other one is that it allows to build according to proven needs without having to bother too much about reserve storage space. Empty

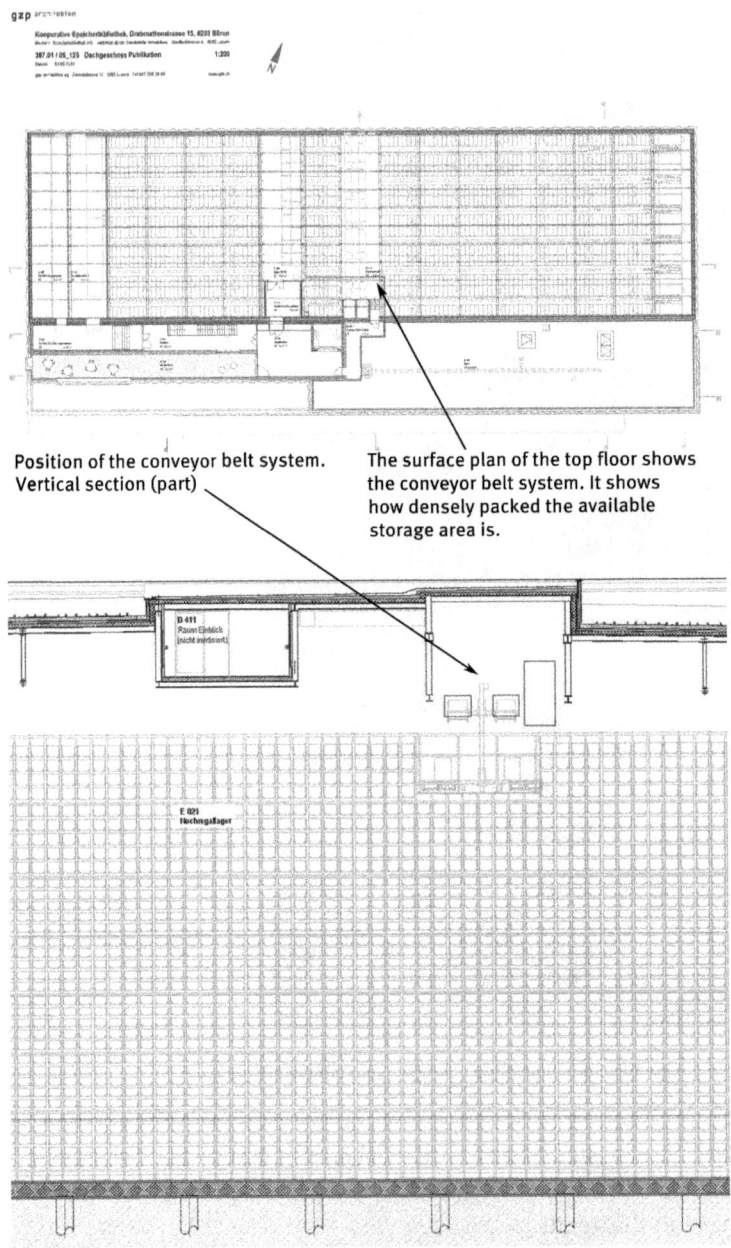

Position of the conveyor belt system.
Vertical section (part)

The surface plan of the top floor shows
the conveyor belt system. It shows
how densely packed the available
storage area is.

Figure 7: plan of surface top floor, and section through storage area.
© gzp Architects, Luzern (Switzerland)

Figure 8: The ground to the right of the CSLS (approx. to the end of the white building) belongs to the plc: potential space for extensions.

space is very expensive! In order to ensure modularity, the plc bought a real estate lot which allows adding three and a half modules of the same size as the existing one, bringing total potential capacity up to 14 mio volumes. But future modules can have different sizes, and they could be fitted with varying climate control units. Thus they could be adapted to different kinds of material.

When planning the existing building, the architects suggested to construct the administrative and HVAC part (which sits in front of the storage part) in the same length and height dimensions as the storage part (its width is only half the width of the storage part). It gave the CSLS one welcome advantage apart from its architectural quality and simplicity: HVAC as well as the Administration have enough space to grow, as there is ample space e.g. for adding further HVAC machinery; for the administration, there is a whole floor where more picking station could be added very quickly.

In fact, the whole building is conceived in a way that makes adding *extensions* as easy as possible: a storage module, for example, could be constructed and outfitted completely independently, without disturbing operations in the existing modules – at the very end one could open the prepared slot in the wall of the existing module, connect the conveyor belt system, and start operations.

Oxygen reduction in the storage area was one of the basic – and very persuasive – principles from the very beginning. The fact that up to now only one other library uses it for its storage protection served to underline the aspect of advanced technology; that this one library is the British Library did not diminish

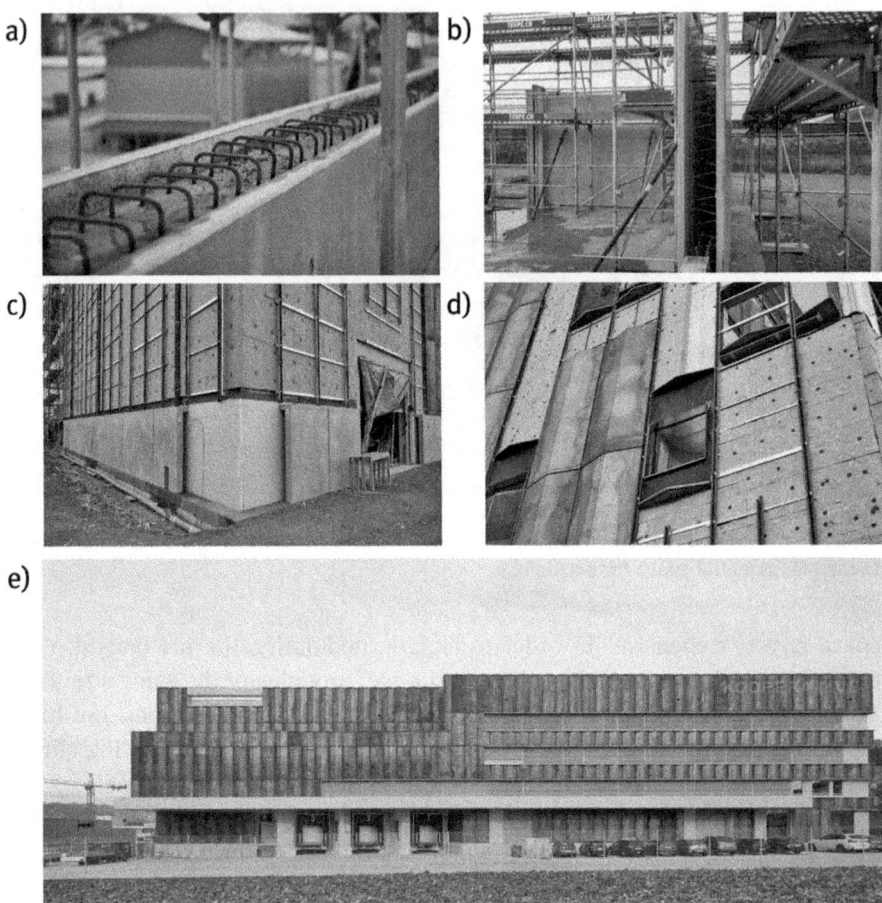

Figure 9: Wall construction: a) Solid concrete, b) Prefabricated sandwich elements, c) Insulation, d) Façade elements added, e) Finished façade

the persuasive power at all... It also helped that oxygen reduction seems to become more of an industry standard for storage buildings (fruit storage, carpenter accessories, automotive parts, etc.). – Oxygen has a concentration of some 21% in our natural environment (ca 200 m above sea level); the storage area of the CSLS has a concentration of around 13.5%, i.e. ca. 4'000 m above sea level. According to Swiss working regulations everyone going into the storage area on a regular basis has to pass an annual health check – a condition for every member of the staff (except the administration person and temporary personnel)!

Figure 10: Empty storage area with HVAC ducts installed

Climate control should also be as reduced as possible, even for the storage area; "passive climate control" was the guideline notion. The most important means to achieve this are massive concrete walls (36 cm for the storage area, 25 cm for the administrative part of the building); 10 to 20 cm insulation were added on its outer side before the external façade which consists of solid Corten steel plates in a folded structure.

HVAC was planned to achieve the preservation conditions that were set at the beginning (18° Celsius, +/– 2°; 45% rel. humidity, +/– 5%). There were long discussions about the complexity to reach these figures, during which it became clear that very slow changes were most important and that a priority was on humidity, it was suggested that more flexible values for temperature would make better sense: temperature could move between 7° and 25° Celsius but not change more than 1° up or down during 24 hours throughout the whole storage area. Conditions for relative humidity were kept: 45 % +/– 5 %. Modelling the need for active HVAC based on the meteorological data of the last ten years showed a need for cooling on one day and for heating on two days per year. Therefore it was decided – with all participating libraries consenting – not to use active HVAC, but to control the climate closely, and to prepare the building for easy installation of all HVAC machinery should it prove necessary.

Sensors for temperature and humidity control are placed throughout the storage area, in high and low positions, and also in containers which are moved around. Figures for the first 18 months show perfectly fulfilled expectations: temperature started at a low 10° Celsius in February 2016 and rose very slowly towards 24° Celsius during late summer 2016 to go down very slowly towards winter. Even in the fairly cold winter of 2016/17 it never went below 10° Celsius. Relative humidity behaved in a similar way: although it started fairly high, it was at the prescribed level in March 2016 and stayed well within the limits. Here the infusion of nitrogen used to reduce oxygen certainly helped: nitrogen is known to reduce relative humidity. We even feared that because of the permanent use of nitrogen relative humidity might be too low in the long run. But up to now, these values behaved well... Finally, air tightness of the storage area was achieved by applying a special coat of paint to the inside walls – it turned into a enormous white, cathedral like space (see Figure 10)! Air tightness is quite successful: instead of the prognosticated ten hours the nitrogen plant runs for just two to three hours a day, most often on standby, to keep the oxygen level on the prescribed level!

Sustainable use of energy is pursued in several ways: first, piles had to be used to prepare the ground for the massive weight (4'000 kg per m2); the piles have a diameter of 50 cm and are 25 m long. Of the 256 piles 60 were used for geothermal heating / cooling of the administrative part of the building; also the heat generated by the nitrogen production is used for heating. Finally, there is a photovoltaic installation on the roof of the whole building, which produces more than 160'000 kWh/a. 80% are used by the CSLS itself; with it, the CSLS has covered close to 100% of its own need in the first seven months of 2017.

Economics: how is it paid for?

Defining the economic side of the CSLS turned out to be fairly easy, especially compared to the process of finding the political framework. It was clear very early on that the CSLS was to be an independent institution, not only from the point of view of organization but also of finances: The participating libraries were to pay all costs: capital costs (i.e. mortgage in form of rent, and depreciation of equipment and building), maintenance costs, and operation costs. There are two basic categories of cost: costs connected with the building and the scope of storage, and costs for processes or operations.

It was equally clear that costs for building and storage should be based on the space an institution wants to reserve for its storage needs (we called it 'reserved room'); empty space and administrative space should be calculated in proportion to the reserved room. Operation costs should be based on the number of actual operations or processes a library causes with its orders.

'Reserved room' proves to be a simple and stable measure; it depends entirely on the library's declared intention. Of course, this figure was also necessary to plan the size of the building, it has therefore been finalized some four years ago. Operations figures were based on estimates of the libraries; they will be checked and updated only after a year of normal business, i.e. after all registered holdings have been ingested. Till then, the CSLS bases its bills on the estimates of the libraries.

Perhaps the most difficult aspect of finances lies in the fact that the CSLS calculations are based on a full cost analysis. This is something not all libraries know or are used to: e.g. they pay no rent for their buildings or space because buildings are owned by the funding body, or because rent is administered centrally. Or they don't know depreciation, because, again, that is calculated in a central administration. It occurred more than once that the planning group and later the CSLS had to defend seemingly high calculations – in most cases it was exactly this difference in calculating with or not with full costs. This is understood well by now – but we fully expect to have the same discussions with new partners!

Conclusion

The CSLS provides support for libraries and users alike. The support for libraries is quite clear-cut:
- it guarantees a safe and stable long-term solution for storing and archiving material,
- this in turn makes it possible to free space for user-focused services in buildings situated in city-centres,
- it allows libraries to save space and costs through de-duplication;
- It provides clear and transparent costs.

Planning and realizing the CSLS was a most fascinating task, instructive on many levels. It was also a very complex and intensive project that sometimes taxed capacities to the limit. The result is a marvellous building which impresses many visitors with its advanced technology (that works most of the time quite smoothly) and with its integrated services to the participating libraries. But the most important achievement, beyond a doubt, is the fact that it was possible to bring high-level cooperation across cantons to life. Because of this, it has significant potential to become an even more important player in the landscape of Swiss librarianship.

Figure 11: The building in summer 2016

Facts and figures

Building measurements	outside	76 m (L) x 35 m (W) x 20 m (H)
	inside (storage)	70 m (L) x 21 m (W) x 15 m (H shelving)
	administration	70 m (L) x 12 m (W) x 18 m (H) + 2.5 m (W) for the roof over the entrance and delivery zone

Capacity: The first module has a capacity of 3.1 mio volumes in 110'000 containers
Additional modules can constructed on the real estate lot, up to a capacity of 14 mio volumes: modules can vary in size and also in climate control conditions.

All libraries except the ZHB Luzern store little use material, the ZHB Luzern stores all its holdings (except open access material and special collections). It is for this reason that Lucerne is the biggest partner library and that it also causes up to 80% of all processes.

Courier service: Once a day, except ZHB Luzern: it has its own courier between the CSLS and Lucerne that runs twice daily

Containers: 60 cm (L) × 40 cm (W); two heights: 25 cm or 35 cm; plastic. On average, a container holds 29 volumes. Its maximum weight must not exceed 60 kg.

Oxygen reduction: Oxygen in the storage area is reduced to 13.5% so as to prevent fire.

Climate control: Temperature: between 7° and 25°, but change not more than 1° in 24 hours; Humidity: 45 %, +/− 5%.

Personnel: core staff of 7 people (1 CEO, 1 in administration, 3.5 in logistics, 0.5 in facility management, 1 librarian). Additional temporary personnel when needed.

Finance figures: Construction incl. real estate costs: CHF 32.5 mio (~$32.5 mio)

Contact: Kooperative Speicherbibliothek Schweiz, Grabmattenstrasse 15, CH-6233 Büron CEO: Mike Märki (mike.maerki@speicherbibliothek.ch) or the author: Ulrich Niederer (ulrich_niederer@bluewin.ch)

Christian Oesterheld

7 Supporting users: ensuring access while preserving archival copies

The users' point of view investing a library storage and automation project

When the idea of the CSLS was developed, the focus was on the lack of the physical space in the participating libraries that would be necessary in order to back up their institutional archiving commitments and to enable them to store their physical items which will be acquired in the future. As the great majority of these libraries is situated in prime locations in the urban centers where the acquisition of supplementary real estate has become unaffordable, growing on their local premises was no option. So the expectation of cost effectiveness looming large behind the idea of a central storage library situated outside city centres could convince political decision makers that this would be a sustainable investment to guarantee physical preservation in a safe infrastructure while making economies of space through reducing duplicate copies between libraries. With this, supporting libraries was a key asset of the CSLS project right from the start.

Not as much focus was put on questions dealing with the consequences for access to the content: indeed, a need was recognized for a broad assessment of users' expectations and, consequently, for the planning of the operational processes which interact with library customers. This perspective was given growing importance during the unfolding of the project. Of course, getting the CSLS constructed remained a foremost preoccupation until the inauguration of the building, as were the planning and implementation of the technically challenging logistics of an automated storage facility which had to be connected to library management systems. But soon we understood that we should be equally concerned about users' services as early as possible.

Patterns of use for a shared journal collection

The decision to situate the CSLS outside the metropolitan areas was tied to the consequence that if physical access was to be granted to readers, they would have to move some 30 km from central Switzerland's capital Lucerne to the location of the storage facility in order to get in touch with the stored items. Consequently, we decided that the standard way to give users access to the content

https://doi.org/10.1515/9783110535372-007

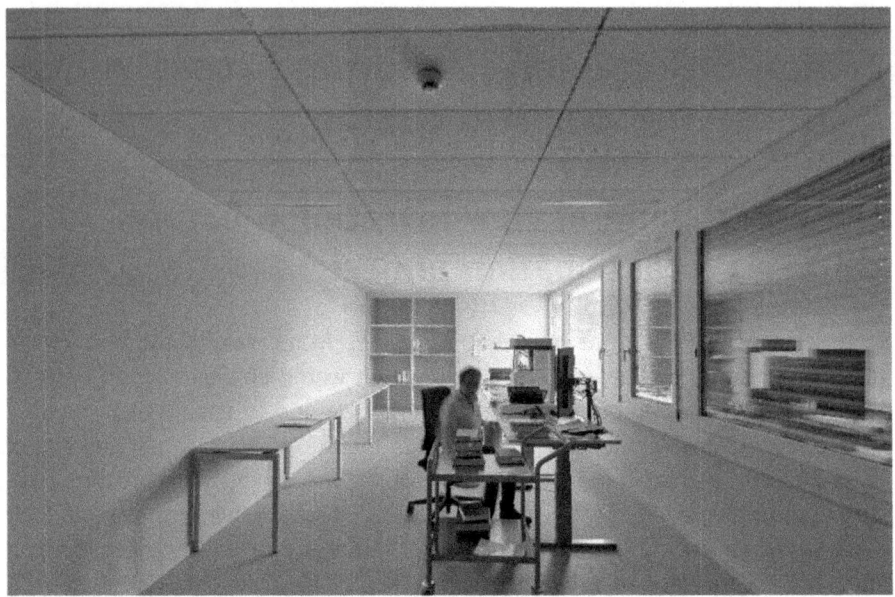

Figure 1: The document delivery scan room at the CSLS.

would be electronic document delivery and courier shipping. Whereas document delivery by scanning articles on demand is available for all items in the CSLS, only the individual holdings of participating libraries are lent physically and can be ordered by users through the courier service. For the shared collection consisting (as for now) of deduplicated printed journal volumes whose ownership has been legally transfered to the CSLS association, the project partners agreed that these items, as a rule, should not leave the CSLS once they had been added to its stocks. Two motifs were behind this decision which turned out to be not very popular with some of our library customers: Firstly, as deduplication was applied to the shared collection, the remaining item will be the only copy preserved among the partner libraries (which are free to remove the duplicate copies from their own stacks), so the safety of this last item is crucial – and any lending inevitably involves some risk of loss or deterioration. Secondly, as there remains only this copy, its availability for document delivery orders must be guaranteed at any time.

As far as we talk about individual holdings of libraries, storing books in the CSLS is equivalent to having them stored in any off-site deposit, the only difference being that the deposit is not operated by the library itself and that it makes use of an advanced technology of automated storage and retrieval. But

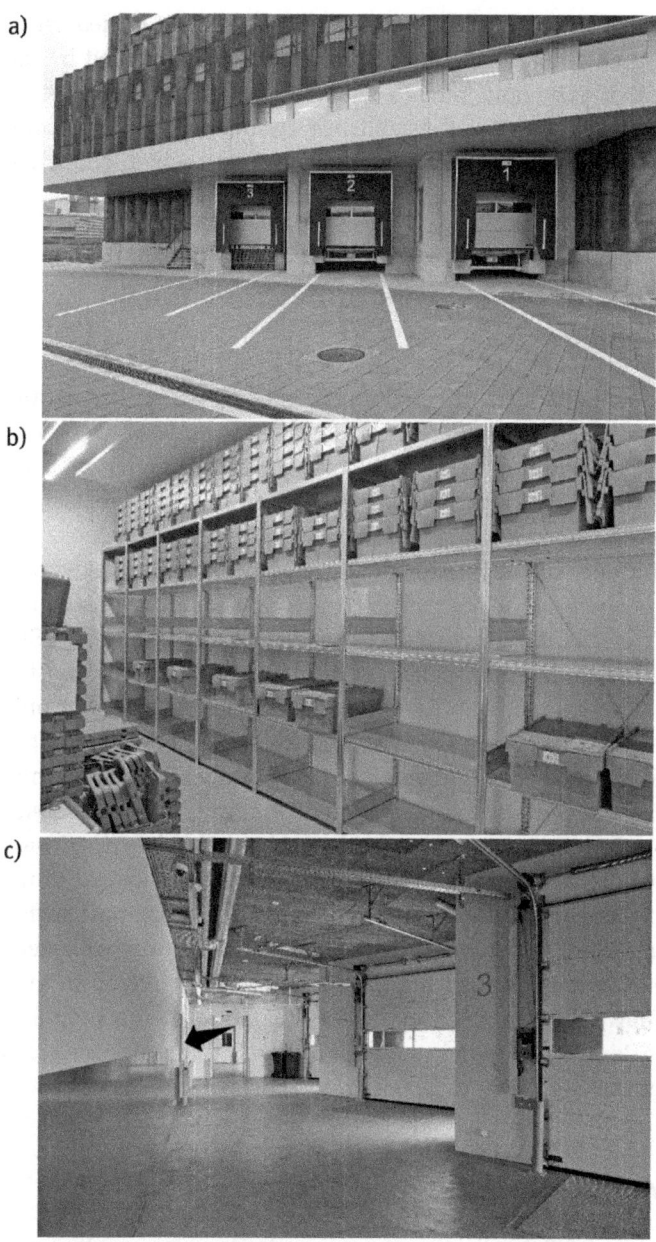

Figure 2: a) CSLS, the delivery area, outside. Access for courier and postal services is via the stairs on the left. b) CSLS, the courier room in the delivery area. c) The delivery area at the CSLS, with 24/7 access possibilities for courier and postal services. The arrow shows the entrance to the courier room.

as far as supplying these items to readers is concerned, there is no reason to restrict shipping and circulation. Thus, lending conditions are governed by the rules of the individual library (and remain generally unchanged). For these holdings we took advantage of the well established courier service connecting the main university libraries of German-speaking Switzerland which cooperate in the IDS network (Informationsverbund Deutschschweiz).

Optimizing logistics for the network through the CSLS: the courier service hub

There was truly a double advantage of coupling the existing courier infrastructure to the new player CSLS: The service is already well-known with users, it is easy to access via direct end-user order from the online catalogs and it offers an attractive price (CHF 5.- per book). Some libraries do not bill their users when they order books from the library's individual holdings in the CSLS. Books are shipped to the home library of the user or to any other library that takes part in the courier service, where he or she can fetch it in the same way as copies from his own library's stacks. By using this existing service structure, the CSLS partners were relieved from creating their own delivery service. Moreover, the CSLS was defined as the logistics hub for the entire courier system: Not only the items stored in the CSLS are loaded here to the IDS courier, but the logistics centre of CSLS is used by the service provider as place of over-night transshipment for all destinations served. Being able to grant 24/7 access to the service provider was therefore one important point in the architect's brief. A software tool allows tracking of the bins from the moment when they are loaded to the vehicle until arrival in the library. The new hub has allowed for time-saving effects, which have resulted in over-night delivery for the majority of orders; when ordered in the afternoon, items from the CSLS will be delivered to their destination the next day. Thus, the CSLS, perfectly situated in the geographical centre of German-speaking Switzerland, now connects all the main university libraries from Basle in the Northwest to St Gall in the East.

Limits of effective use by way of remote services

Whereas the distant use of CSLS collections was conceived as the standard way of access for users, we understood during the planning process of operations that for some scenarios of use, it could be helpful to consult the physical items on-site. This concerns mainly the collective journal holdings, which are not

Figure 3: The reading room at the CSLS.

available via the courier service. The possibility to order a scan of a given article sometimes does not meet users' requirements effectively. This is particularly true for bibliograpic and historiographic research, when readers wish to browse through the complete series of issues of a given journal title in order to verify bibliographic references or, for example, follow the development of a much debated topic through the publication history of one or multiple journals. The importance of this kind of research with journals varies between disciplines, and it is true that the approach of literary criticism as a key to contemporaneous research discussions defends its value in the humanities, whereas it has rather faded away in the exact and applied sciences. So even if this use of journal material does not prevail among the vast majority of users, it remains very important for some of them. That is why a reading room in the CSLS building was provided for, where holdings which would not go out of the deposit may be consulted by users. They register for their visit with their home library, which in turn informs the CSLS staff about the items to prepare. In this way, readers can access even huge quantities of material in an effective way. Another motif for autopsy can be the search for and the work with illustrations, which require a close look at the original. For this, a standard text scan is often not satisfactory. Besides the possibility to access the volumes in the reading room of the

CSLS, the partners agreed that to this effect it should be possible to transfer the items – via an internal lending process – to the specialised reproduction departments of the libraries in order to produce high-resolution scans of illustrations.

Yet, we had to admit that some of our readers still felt uncomfortable with the removal of the printed journals to an off-site storage facility. The effects of this differ locally, because the outsourcing strategies of the participating libraries were not identical. Some libraries transferred more or less their complete holdings of print journals to the collective deposit due to storage limitations on their local premises. Users of these libraries who were accustomed to browse through the print volumes in open stacks found the transfer from the local shelves to the CSLS to be a rather disruptive experience. Other libraries had the possibility to make a selection of which titles should be deposited and which ones could be kept in the library, because their local storage capacity was still sufficient to retain at least part of their journal holdings. The method employed for the selection process varied from intellectually based decisions per title made by subject specialist librarians to (un)blocking a whole range of titles for deposit according to either systematic shelving or classificatory elements contained in the metadata.

As already stated above, it is difficult to estimate the relative proportion of critical voices against the total number of active users, most of whom do not comment on the change. But we have to acknowledge that there is a group of users who struggle with the newly limited access to the physical journal volumes. They feel that the absence of the browsing mode of access is an obstacle to the famous serendipity experience they pretend to have had in the open journals stacks. Often, they state, it is difficult to find exact bibliographic data of articles especially of older journal material as these data have not been incorporated in general bibliographic databases or not even in subject specific bibliographies, nor are they included in the article indexes of today's discovery systems. So they claim that they simply do not know which article to order as a document scan, if they cannot discover the journal contents by browsing the corresponding volumes. And it is true that tables of contents are often not available via the internet, publishers' sites or library catalogs for older journal issues and even for contemperanous issues of rather spezialized journals with limited target groups. We also heard some objections that "locking away" the journals would impede not only research, but also academic training inasfar as faculty allegedly cannot give anymore essays to students in which they have to outline the development of an intellectual concept or a historiographically significant idea through the publication stream of a certain period.

What is a "journal" from the cataloguer's point of view – and what about the consequences for users?

A specific feature of serials in the cataloger's perspective is the wavering border line between journals in the commonly established sense of the term on the one hand, i.e. a periodical scholarly publication containing a number of separate articles of individual authors, and multi-volume publications of monographic or encyclopedic caracter as well as monographs embedded in a numbered series on the other hand which formally have been catalogued and shelfmarked as journals on the basis of their continuous volume count and of having been published at more or less regular intervals. This practice seems to have been particularly characteristic of the German cataloguing tradition. Typically, monograph series published by academies of sciences or similar organizations as well as single works published as (only formally dependent) supplements to a journal have been catalogued as journal issues. In theses cases, there are often no individual title records in the catalogs which would help to identify the de-facto-monographic pieces or, if such entries exist, they have not been linked to the journals' main record. Sometimes the conversion of old card catalogs was defective as to this aspect. So when the lists of items for the transfer to the central deposit were drawn up, it was almost predictable that a huge number of these entities would not be identified as the "pseudo-journals" they are in reality.

As a consequence, attention will often be focused on these items only when a user actually searches for them in the online catalogue and shows up at the help desk complaining that he is unwilling to order a scan because it is the entire volume he needs to see or, alternatively, just some small pieces of text dispersed throughout a longer monograph or miscellanous work. For the user, there is the question of costs involved with the scan order, but also the standard limitation for scans we had to fix due to copyright legislation: scans must not exceed 75% of the content of a complete work still under copyright protection (whereas single articles of a journal or miscellaneous volume can be reproduced integrally). In order to meet better our readers' requirements, we decided that for these difficult instances we would deviate from the general non-lending policy defined for the collective journal repository and permit short-term loan of items for consultation under surveillance in the reading rooms of participating libraries. This should allow for a more convenient use of content while sustaining the preservation and security needs for the unified journal holdings.

Enhancing access by digitizing tables of contents and full texts: some reflections

As the complaint about the unavailability of tables of contents which would allow readers to target a given journal article seemed justified for quite a number of academic journals, we considered a digitization project of journal tables of contents not found in our catalogues or somewhere on the web for free, which would center around the collective holdings of the CSLS. As a powerful scan operating infrastructure was implemented in the CSLS in order to have a swift document delivery workflow, the technical infrastructure to process mass scanning of ToCs is already in place. Yet, given the important financial resources in terms of staff and IT repository infrastructure necessary to cover a representative layer of titles, user needs must be evaluated carefully. There are probably also copyright issues to be solved. Anyway, it would be a waste of money and time to scan ToCs which are already elsewhere on the web or, alternatively, could be purchased and loaded to our repository. Identifying these titles turned out to be a laborious and time-consuming task, which can hardly be done automatically due to the lack of unified metadata sources. This is particularly true for hybrid journals of which only recent volumes have been published digitally, whereas the archives of the preceding issues are not covered by the electronic edition. And even where the complete series of a given journal is available electronically, but the e-edition is not published open access, there may be only a partial overlap between the actual licences of the participating libraries to the effect that access is restricted. And finally, would giving access to ToCs – without doubt an improvement if compared to the present situation – really be a satisfactory solution for users? What they really want is full-text access, to be able to read a page or two of an article in order to be sure if they want to proceed or in order to verify a citation, a scattered footnote somewhere and so on. So this project of massive scanning of ToCs is still being examined, not a least with respect to raising the funds for realisation.

The best answer to users' needs without any doubt would be an effort in full-text digitization of journal content. It seems preferable to engage for broadening retrodigitization of academic journals, notably those in languages other than English and covering specialized topics of the humanities, which have less chances to be included on their own in the big aggregator archives. There are open access digitization initiatives for domestic academic journals in several countries, for exemple the project e-periodica.ch in Switzerland, and publishing houses too add continuously older volumes to their e-archives, which can be licensed. Besides this, JSTOR is certainly the most relevant aggregator archive for academic journals, which has built a broad coverage of journal backfiles.

Thus, it would be interesting to have included certain backfiles of core journal titles which are archived among the CSLS collective holdings and are not yet present in the JSTOR collections.

Print archiving and availability of electronic backfiles

When establishing the lists of titles selected for transferral to the CSLS, it might have seemed obvious to verify if all the journals on the list are available in digital editions. Yet, as already stated, at least some of the participating libraries in reality had no choice to exclude titles published exclusively in print format, because lack of space in their own buildings forced them to withdraw their complete journal collection. But what is more interesting is the fact that a reliable match print/electronic is a very complex project to obtain on a title basis if you have to deal with some 10'000 journal titles or more and do not want to process this huge amount of data intellectually.

The reasons for this challenge are multiple: Evidence in the library catalogues is heterogenous, as many libraries still have not included all their licensed journals in the main online catalogue, or, even if they have, the matches are not always unambiguous. Even more difficult is the case with Open Access journals which also often have not been systematically added to the traditional library catalogues. Often journals with a long-running publication history are split between an earlier series not yet digitized and the more recent digital born issues. After all, identifying the online availability of academic journal titles is often equivalent to hitting a moving target, as the overlaps of electronic and print segments constantly change.

Lessons learnt: the need for pragmatic answers to shifting users' needs

What, then, did we learn from the first two years of operation of the CSLS from the point of view of our users? First we would argue that, in a sense, as librarians we probably went a bit too far in what we believed to be the evolving needs of the academic clientele we serve. At least in the humanities, the shift in the journals ecosphere towards electronic formats has not yet been as complete as one might expect. Perhaps we might be blamed for not having systematically checked our print journal holdings against the availability of e-journal equivalents (even if, as argued in more detail above, there are substantial methodological and practical problems to such an approach). Yet without any doubt the shift *is* taking place, be it with relative differences of pace according to disciplines, and so we can be optimistic that readers' concerns, if not disappearing completely, at least will diminish, to the effect that in the long run the collective journal holdings of the CSLS will foremost have the role of an archive serving long-term preservation of the print heritage of academic journals.

For the time being, as long as fully digitized backfiles are not available for the whole range of journal titles, we will go on adapting practice regulations to users' needs while striving for a balance with the archival principles of the CSLS. Making accessible some material in the local reading rooms which by former regulations would not have been 'lendable' was a first step into this direction. Furthermore, it would be a very attractive service for users if article copies made on demand could be put permanently at the disposal of all users via the online catalogues in due course, as it is current practice e.g. with the E-Books on Demand service for copyright free monographs. However this would entail copyright clearance for each article (which must be free not only of author's copyright, but also of publishers' rights) and also the need for creating catalog records of the articles to have them included in the online catalogues. Nurturing a still bolder idea, one could imagine an endeavor of massive full text digitization of all the copyright free journal issues in the central deposit. As with the table of contents project discussed above, this would require careful scrutiny for each item about its online availability in order to avoid futile retrodigitization. Complementing the free content with those titles which are formally still under copyright but do not represent any more an economic interest for their publishers once again would require careful one-by-one copyright clearance and mutual agreements with publishers – and, of course, substantial funding. But the material preconditions for such an enterprise would be ideal with the operational prerequisites being in place with the scan production facility in the CSLS and, first of all, with what is in fact a widely aggregated journals repository with representative holdings of the major academic serials which laid the ground for research in Europe throughout the 19th and 20th century.

Enlarging the scope of the CSLS: new perspectives from the Swiss Library Service Platform

Currently a project is under way in Switzerland which aims at creating a Swiss national library service agency supporting libraries in their basic workflows. This project will lead to full operation of the Swiss Library Service Platform (SLSP) by 2020/2021. In the design phase of the SLSP project a rich and detailed service catalogue with a varied portfolio of basic and optional services designed for academic libraries in Switzerland has been developed. Whereas at the center of SLSP we will find a new cloud-based library management system – and during 2017 much attention has been focused on the procurement of this backbone infrastructure –, there are some elements in the future service portfolio which point to a possible role of the CSLS at the national scale. So the function of the central logistics hub of the courier service connecting today the university libraries of the German-speaking part of Switzerland could be extended to a national hub. Geography and scalability would favour choosing the CSLS for this hub, and the current courier service solution has well proven its operability. SLSP, according to the service catalogue which was elaborated during the project, will build a courier service on a national scale and unite the hitherto unconnected shipping services of the existing multi-network structure.

With new clients from the larger SLSP community who may whish to join the CSLS and for this need to rely upon an enlarged storage facility, the shared journal collection of the CSLS could truly become a comprehensive yet de-duplicated archive of print journals held by all the major academic libraries of Switzerland. This would offer a sustainable long-term solution for the infrastructure of archiving institutions most of which face serious problems over sufficient local storage space, and it could be an efficient answer to document delivery and digitization needs. And why not follow the example of the current UK Research Reserve initiative and think about an extension of the concept by creating a central research monograph reserve built from the printed monograph collections which the libraries are ready to contribute to a shared and de-duplicated collection, prioritising older and specialized material? The experience gathered from de-duplication of journal holdings in the CSLS and from the balancing of preservation goals with actual users' needs could help to achieve a solution which meets cost effectiveness and the need for a secure backfile of research collections which were built over generations on the one hand and smooth access to a broad content on the other while taking into account the evolution of researchers' needs in an integrated digital working environment.

Conclusion

The CSLS provides support for libraries and users alike. Support for users is fairly evident from the point of view of the libraries:
- users profit from newly freed space
- within their on-site library, they see the most up-to-date holdings more clearly, uncluttered by too many books that could not be placed elsewhere;
- the library has capacity to develop new services instead of having to fight for the means for constructing new space.

Figure 4: The CSLS is off-site, in the countryside, not in a city centre. Distances from Büron to Luzern: 30 km, to Zürich: 75 km, to Basel: 80 km, to St. Gall: 145 km.

But from the point of view of the users themselves,

- an off-site storage of whatever kind "robs" them of holdings they wish to have immediate access to – they cannot browse holdings extensively and on site as before;
- they have to pay for document delivery of articles they formerly could copy themselves.

These are important points, especially where the interaction between libraries and users is concerned. Right now there is a tendency that users complain to their home libraries which chose to participate in the shared collection and blame the CSLS for their difficulties to consult holdings "as they always did". These complaints are often underpinned with a general criticism of the de-duplication of holdings. This is a problem well known – there are numerous reports of comparable difficulties wherever off-site storage becomes a necessity. But that does not help in an actual case. We'll have to find a positive way to resolve these difficulties, in particular find a better solution for users used to browsing especially journals directly on the shelf.

On a more general level, the CSLS itself is an institution of cooperation. With its character as a centralized service platform, it is ideally placed to interact with the collaborative approach followed nowadays in Swiss academic libraries, especially with the important Swiss Library Service Platform (SLSP).

Jonny Edvardsen and Helen Sakrihei

8 The Repository Library

The Norwegian Repository library is a part of the National Library of Norway (NLN). When the NLN was established in Mo i Rana in 1989 the Repository Library was one of the first functions to become operative from the new institution. At the time of the opening, a Repository Library had been a function long awaited in Norwegian libraries. The arguments for this function were threefold:
- streamlining document delivery
- providing the libraries with a stable and enduring access to older materials
- saving resources for the local libraries because centralized storing makes it easier to discard low-use material already stored in a Repository Library

As an element in the establishing of NLN the Norwegian Parliament passed a new Legal Deposit act in June 1989. The Repository Library is included in this act, stating that one of the seven legal deposit copies in Norway is intended for interlibrary loan (ILL), and placed in the Repository Library. This provision secures the inclusion of a large amount of new publications to the Repository Library, in addition to all the old material transferred from the local libraries all around Norway.

During the first ten years from the opening in 1989 the Repository Library used traditional shelving for the collection. The material was arranged by acquisition number and placed in compact shelving. The use and administration of the collection was time consuming, and when the need of an expansion of the storage facilities emerged around year 2000, the management found an opportunity to replan the Repository Library. The storage principle was changed from the old staff-to-material to the new material-to-staff. This shift was made possible by the implementation of an Automatic storage and Retrieval System (ASRS), which utilises miniload cranes for handling and storing of the library material in steel bins.

Functions of the Repository Library

The Repository Library is an integrated part of the Norwegian Library landscape, performing important services for all libraries:
- The main node in the interlending network
- Central mass storage for little used material

https://doi.org/10.1515/9783110535372-008

- Secures the "last ILL copy" in Norway
- Main point for digitization of Norwegian books
- Norwegian International Standard Identifier for *Libraries* and Related Organisation (ISIL) agency

The interlending network in Norway is functioning quite well. Nearly all libraries participate, including both public and academic libraries. The network facilitates use of all library material regardless of library. A patron is able to get hold of most of the material either as a physical item, as a digital file via e-mail, or as a browsable digital copy accessible in the reading room of the local library.

The Repository Library has been an important part of this strategy since the establishment in 1989, and has been the biggest ILL contributor in Norway for several years. It is estimated that 25% of all the ILL material is delivered from the Repository Library.

The national policy in Norway concerning ILL is based on short transport and efficient handling. The material is registered in online catalogues, and the first searches for an interlending copy is done in the catalogues of the nearby libraries. If no copy is found there, the next place to search is the Repository Library. From 2017 this process is automated, and the search is done in a central database established for the purpose.

One of the main Repository Library functions is to secure access to low-use material in a cost-effective way. In Norway books older than 4–5 years has a steep decline in use. Material older than 10-20 years has a very low but stable use. Until the Repository Library was established in 1989 each Library had to decide whether a book should be kept or discarded. Usually too many libraries kept the same material. At the same time, there were no mechanisms securing that not all copies of important books were discharged. The on-line catalogue of the Repository Library is an easy way for libraries to check if the material they want to discard is kept for interlending. If there are too few copies in the Repository the library can transfer their copy, if there are enough books kept centrally they can discard their material.

In 2005 the National Library of Norway decided that all Norwegian material in the collection should be digitized. The decision was partly based on concern about long time preservation, but digitization would also give opportunities for instant access and free text search that would facilitate use of the collection. The Repository Library has been an integrated part of the digitization strategy since the beginning. The large and central collection is an efficient starting point for digitization. Automatic handling of orders and a very efficient picking of copies for scanning has made it possible for the Repository to deliver 1 000 copies a week for scanning. Until now more than 450 000 books are digitized. In a couple of years from now all Norwegian books will be scanned, and the work will continue with periodicals.

The Repository Library is in charge of allocation and maintenance of the ISIL as the National Registration Allocation Agency in Norway. Every Library in Norway is given an ISIL-number, which is used in the interlending network.

Figure 8.1: The storage capacity of the automatic storages is 2.5 million publications. Photo: The National Library of Norway.

The ASRS

Implementation of the Automated Storage and Retrieval System (ASRS) in 2003 marked a substantial shift for the Repository Library. The ASRS is an automatic miniload storage facility, based on the principle of "object to operator". There are several reasons why NLN chose this technology. Wages are high in Norway, encouraging automation of manual workflows. The ASRS is very efficient, enabling staff to dispatch a much larger amount of orders with the same amount of man-hours, compared with an ordinary library setup. The building used for an ASRS is cost-effective. You need a large and open storage facility for the material, in addition to the ordinary workspace for the staff. The construction of buildings in Norway is expensive, so although the storage facility must be fitted with cranes and conveyors for handling the material and thousands of bins and steel shelving for the bins, the overall cost was less than a conventional building with rooms, floors and compact shelving.

The Ministry of Culture in Norway has defined efficient handling of ILL orders as one of the central goals for NLN. The target is that 95% of the orders should be dispatched within 24 hours. The use of ASRS is instrumental in fulfilling this goal.

The idea of using ASRS in the Repository Library surfaced with the need for expansion of the premises around the year 2000. Calculations showed that building of an automatic storage would be cheaper than an ordinary building and it would also demand less staff. The National Library in Mo i Rana has from the start been well equipped with technical staff, as a result of being located in an industrial town. This fact probably made it easier for the library administrators to consider such a dramatic shift in technology. Before the final decision several sites in Europe which had implemented ASRS were visited, including libraries, banks and goods handling facilities in a more industrial setting.

Storage in the ASRS is done in a quite advanced way, compared with other facilities. Each object is equipped with a barcode. The physical storage is done in steel bins, each marked with a barcode. In every bin there are a number of folders, also marked with unique barcodes. Storing an object involves the process of retrieving a bin from the stacks, reading the barcode on the object which is going to be stored, placing the object in a folder, and reading the barcode on the folder. The rest is taken care of by the warehouse system. The system knows where the bin should be stored, it keeps track of which folder holds the book, and the connection between the folder and the bin. It also has the ability for shuffle bins with low-used material to the back of the store, in an automated way. Each bin contains just one material type, and storage in the stacks is independent of the content of the bin.

To store the items efficiently there are 3 different bin sizes, and 4 different folder sizes (one type of bin holds two types of folders). The sizes and number of folders of each size are based on historical data showing the sizes of published books in Norway.

The sizes of the folders are in millimetres (the quantity of each size in %):

- Type 1: 253 × 173 mm (33%)
- Type 2: 253 × 235 mm (30%)
- Type 3: 370 × 235 mm (30%)
- Type 4: 369 × 355 mm (7%)

An expansion of the ASRS was done in 2015. The new ASRS uses the same technology as the old one, and the capacity was expanded from 1,5 million to 2,5 million books. After the expansion the stacks now contain 72 000 steel bins.

Every morning at 07:00, all orders received during the last 24 hours are transferred automatically from the library systems (Alma and Bibliofil) to the warehouse system. This ensures that all single orders to a specific library are combined into a merged order before picking. When the staff arrives at 08:00 the first bins are waiting at the picking stations, and the orders are retrieved until 12:30. The material is then dispatched through the mail. The rest of the day the ASRS can be used for storing new material, retrieving journals for article copying, books for digitization or other tasks. The amount of ILL orders vary significantly through the year, but at peak periods over 600 books are dispatched each day.

During 2017 the Multilingual Library was transferred to the repository. The Multilingual Library is a library collection in over 60 different languages. The target group for this collection is asylum seekers, refugees and immigrants.

Figure 8.2: There are 72 000 steel bins in the automatic storages. Photo: The National Library of Norway.

Pros

Installation of the ASRS in Mo i Rana is considered successful. The benefits of utilizing an ASRS include very accurate tracking of each stored item, effective handling of books and other materials, very compact storage (low footprint), possibilities to automate most of the ordering and reduced labour costs.

A major problem in almost every library is keeping track of where the books are at any time. It is easy to misplace a book, and a misplaced book can be very hard to find. Often a minor human error is enough to make a book disappear on the wrong shelf. In the ASRS no book has a fixed place, but the warehouse system keeps track of every book, where it is at any given time, when it is retrieved and if it is used. The only human operation involved is scanning the barcode of the book, and the barcode of the folder. This secures a minimum of possible mistakes, and the number of misplaced objects is less than 0,05% each year. In addition most of the misplaced objects are found in the same bin as they are supposed to be, but in another folder.

The ASRS makes it possible to automate most of the ordering process. Standardized protocols are used for the exchange of ILL messages between the Library system and the warehouse system. This enables the different systems do many mechanical parts of the workflow, like sorting and logistics. The retrieving principle ("object to operator") saves several man-hours just in walking time, and this is one of the factors that makes it possible for the Repository Library to steadily perform a 10% increase in the lending activity without increasing the staff accordingly. Each year nearly 200 000 ILL orders are being fulfilled at the Repository Library. All these objects are being detected, dispatched and retuned back to the warehouse. This is in addition to all new materials that are received and stored, and also in addition to all the books and journals brought out for digitization. No direct cost calculation has been done on how much savings are in staff time from the ASRS, but it is believed to be substantial.

Cons

Picking of books at the ASRS can be a little tedious. The workflow is quite effective, and each operator retrieves over 50 books an hour. The Repository Library has addressed this problem by letting the staff work no more than 3 hours in the ASRS, and then they work the rest of the day with other tasks like acquisition, registration of books and so on.

In 2015 the Repository Library changed the library system, along with nearly all the other academic libraries in Norway. The change proved to be a challenge. The ILL part of the old library system was close connected to the ASRS. The implementation of the new system (Alma from Ex Libris) was very time consuming, and many of the problems experienced were not anticipated. An extra challenge occurred since Norway changed the ILL protocols at the same time, and the interaction between the ASRS, Alma and the rest of the library systems used in Norway was more or less non-existing at the time of the transfer from the old to the new system. The effect of this was that the ILL in the academic libraries in Norway declined the first year after the transfer, and especially the Repository Library had a drop in received orders.

Facts:
The collection:
- 1 200 000 books
- 56 000 microfilms
- 2 300 000 periodical issues
- Some audiobooks, musical recordings and other materials

The collection grows with 50 000 books and 100 000 volumes of periodicals each year.

Use:
100 000 physical copies dispatched each year, will be 160 000 in 2018 because of the inclusion of the Multilingual Library in the collection

Staff: 18 Full-time equivalent

Michael Robinson

9 The past, present and future of a print repository: CAVAL and the changing context for print storage and preservation

Abstract: In 1995, the membership of the Australian library co-operative CAVAL commenced a bold and far-reaching experiment in the management of print collections, with the establishment of the CAVAL Shared Collection. This is a repository of print materials ceded in perpetuity by each member library to the custodianship of CAVAL, to form an archive of research resources for the benefit of present and future generations of students and scholars. In 2010, CAVAL opened a second print repository, this time based on the membership opting for a quite different model of formed collections occupying discrete sections of space on a leased basis, maintaining ownership of these materials and controlling both their access and the duration of their storage offsite. Over twenty years later, two questions are before CAVAL as both repositories approach the end of their available capacity: – does the potential exist for a third print repository, and if so, what form should it take? This chapter reviews the development of the CAVAL print repositories and discusses the opportunities and challenges ahead for print storage.

The Foundation of CAVAL

CAVAL is a not-for-profit library co-operative which was established in 1978 in Victoria, Australia. An acronym for "Co-operative Action by Victorian Academic Libraries", CAVAL originated as a result of a report commissioned by Victorian universities in 1976 to identify opportunities for collaboration amongst their academic libraries. The impetus for this inquiry was to investigate opportunities for efficiencies and cost savings through shared or centralised library cataloguing and technical services. The report concluded that an entity would need to be created to manage technical services collaboratively, and if so this would also open up possibilities for other types of library collaboration. CAVAL was subsequently established as a joint enterprise of Victorian universities and higher education institutions. Almost 40 years later, CAVAL provides a range of services to libraries throughout Australia and New Zealand while still remaining faithful to its mission to provide benefit to member libraries through collaboration.

https://doi.org/10.1515/9783110535372-009

While CAVAL's activities are national in scale, its core membership still consists of all Victorian universities, the one current exception to this being the University of New South Wales. CAVAL's governance consists of a Board of Directors drawn largely from member institutions and sub-committees which oversee the company's services and membership activities, and finance and audit respectively. The CAVAL constitution allows scope for a broad range of activities, principally focussed on working with libraries but also encompassing education, as well as cultural institutions such as museums, galleries and archives.

In its early years, CAVAL focussed its efforts on member co-operative activities, including in particular the establishment and co-ordination of the CAVAL Reciprocal Borrowing Program in 1979, a service to enable staff and students from one member institution to borrow directly from the libraries of other members. Innovative at the time, this service continues to the present day and remains an enduring legacy of the CAVAL initiative which has had direct end user benefit. More co-operative programs followed throughout the 1980's and 90's, and included professional development and networking, training courses in library disaster management and recovery of print collections. Professional communities of practice were established and fostered by CAVAL, in areas such reference research and information services, and library professional development, and these likewise continue through to the present day, providing professional development, networking and learning opportunities for member library staff through conferences, seminars and other programs. A cross-institutional mentoring program which came under CAVAL management in 2011 has fostered over 200 mentoring relationships in the Victorian academic library community.

Following its original brief, CAVAL began to offer shared cataloguing and technical services to its membership on a fee-for-service basis from the early 1980's, and has expanded in this area to become a leader in the supply and cataloguing of Language Other Than English materials, and more recently English Language Teaching resources.

Over an extensive period of time, the company has also been instrumental in supporting a number of interlending and document supply initiatives in Australia and New Zealand, supporting at different stages the Fretwell-Downing LIDDAS system, VDX, and more recently the Relais International suite of products. CAVAL utilizes surpluses from these activities to help sustain the company and its extensive building infrastructure, and to re-invest in new services to support and benefit the membership. The majority of CAVAL's income is from these activities, and alleviates the obligation of the membership to fund the upkeep of facilities and continuation of member programs.

The CARM Centre

The event of greatest consequence for CAVAL in its early history – and a watershed for the future development of the company – was the establishment of a purpose built facility for its operations in 1995. Since its founding, CAVAL had been operating from leased premises in different locations around Melbourne. However, in the early 1990's member libraries resolved to establish a purpose-built offsite storage facility to accommodate print collections which they wished to retain, but no longer needed to be immediately accessible. This led to the design and construction of the CARM (CAVAL Archive and Research Materials) Centre, and alongside it the establishment of the CARM Shared Collection.

The CARM Centre was constructed on a site leased from La Trobe University (a CAVAL member) on its Research and Development Park, and consists of staff and operational accommodation and training and conference facilities, in addition to the purpose-built print storage facility housing approximately 15 linear kilometres of shelving. When conceptualizing the Shared Collection, CAVAL and its membership needed to address several key issues in the long-term retention of print holdings, the first of these being to build a facility which would have the technical capability to maintain optimum storage conditions indefinitely. The storage facility was designed and constructed to exacting standards, to ensure that temperature and humidity controls – necessary for the long-term storage and preservation of print materials – could be maintained into the future, and the facility effectively functions as a large sealed container to maintain a stable environment at minimal cost. The storage facility is also secured and has only one entrance at each level, to ensure that as little disruption as possible occurs to these environmental settings.

The CARM Shared Collection

The project to establish a shared collection of member research materials was driven principally by the membership, and the policies which shaped and governed its subsequent development emerged from an extensive planning and consultative phase undertaken over a three year period. Several key policy and procedural decisions were made in the planning phase, henceforth determining the character and future directions of the Shared Collection, and it is useful to consider these individually. (Jilovsky 2013)

A key aspect of the long-term retention of print is to ensure that the collection is not only secure from a technical perspective (through security, fire and air management systems) but also as a matter of policy. In the case of the CARM

Shared Collection this was underwritten fundamentally by the commitment of the members to hold materials in perpetuity. To achieve this, CAVAL members entered into an agreement to cede to CAVAL ownership of any materials which they transferred into the collection. When member libraries deposit items into the CARM Shared Collection, they have no further claim on the material and no right to return that item to the member library's collections at a later date. As a key part of this commitment, CAVAL is tasked by the members to hold and manage the collection on their behalf, maintaining environmental and other controls for the long-term preservation of the collection.

Through these mechanisms, retention and access to these materials is guaranteed in future. It ensures that the membership can rely on an item being held in the Shared Collection in order that decisions can be made about their own collections, in particular about materials which may duplicate existing holdings at CAVAL. This not only ensures the long-term integrity of the Shared Collection – once deposited, an item can never be discarded – but provides the basis on which other member libraries can with confidence dispose of their own copies of the same item.

Another principle of the Shared Collection is that CAVAL does not impose a specific collection development policy over its members for the materials they introduce into the collection. Instead, participating members are provided with the flexibility of relegating materials into the shared collection according to their own collection policies and judgements, and their own priorities for what is needed locally in the library and what can be transferred permanently to storage. Fundamentally, there are only three key criteria stipulated by the membership for inclusion of items in the Shared Collection. The first of these is that the item must be deemed to have a long-term research value. The second is that materials must be in a suitable condition to enable them to be stored and retrieved over a long period, and therefore free of insect infestation, mould or other physical deterioration which could potentially impact on the rest of the collection. In addition, as the Shared Collection is conceptualised as a "last single copy" collection, libraries must de-duplicate their materials against the Shared Collection's holdings, so as to ensure that only unique materials are deposited.

The CARM Centre (or CARM1 as it is known within the membership) was built through a combination of funding from the Australian Government, the Victorian State Government (via the State Library of Victoria, which was to become a major holder of collections in the storage facility) and funds from each participating member institution. Consequently, CAVAL membership has been allocated space in the Shared Collection proportionate with their contribution of funds in constructing the facility. However, to ensure that the highest density of shelf storage is obtainable, all materials entering the collection are re-processed, allocated their own barcode, which in turn is assigned to a particular packing tray of items with a similar size, and this in turn is allocated a fixed location in the collection. Thus, materials are stored and interfiled in packing trays purely by size, not library of origin, subject or classification. This enables CAVAL to pack the optimum number of items into the collection, adjusting packing trays and shelf height to suit the size of materials to achieve the highest possible density of storage. Materials are retrievable only by the barcode, and these are assigned to holdings statements in the bibliographic record for each item in the collection, managed via CAVAL's in-house library management system. Items in the Shared Collection are searchable via the CAVAL database as well as the Libraries Australia catalogue and in some cases via a link from a member's discovery layer.

Through this combination of factors, funding for the Shared Collection thus comes from three sources. First, members have invested in the construction of the Shared Collection to a greater or lesser degree, for which they receive a proportionate allocation of space. Second, members are charged a processing fee for each item which they enter into the collection, to cover the cost of physical processing and the creation of the bibliographic record. Third, members are levied an annual maintenance fee for the upkeep of the facility according to the extent of the space they have been allocated.

Growth and Usage of the Shared Collection

As anticipated at the time of its establishment, the accumulation of holdings in the Shared Collection has plateaued over its twenty year history, and at present consists of over 850,000 monograph and serial volumes, or approximately 85% of available capacity in the CARM1 storage facility. The period of greatest collection growth was in the ten years following the opening of the CARM Centre, as members transferred a backlog of materials accumulated in anticipation of the storage facility becoming available. Ingest of materials has gradually tapered off over the subsequent fifteen years as member libraries divested themselves of lesser used materials, and collection growth is now less than .5% per annum. In practical terms, while overall 15% capacity remains and is unlikely to be filled for years to come, some member libraries have consumed their allocations, while others have redundant capacity at their disposal. Recognizing this, adjustments have been made to enable members to trade unused space if desired. The Shared Collection was conceived as a low-use collection of research materials, and retrievals annually are in the vicinity of 8000–9000 items, or less than 1%

of the collection overall. Despite this, retrievals have increased over time, with rates of less than 2000 per annum recorded between the first five and ten years of operation.

CARM2 Offsite Storage

Ten years after the opening of CARM1 and the founding of the Shared Collection, the Board of Directors and CAVAL management began to plan for an additional storage facility at the La Trobe University site, anticipating both the ultimate filling of the first facility and a growing need from some members to decant more materials into offsite storage from library collections. However, instead of extending or replicating the existing storage facility and by default the Shared Collection, the CAVAL membership opted for a different model, which responded to their needs and interests in the wake of the Shared Collection experience.

The CARM2 project planned for the construction of a significantly larger print repository, ultimately containing 63 linear kilometres of shelving. Instead of continuing with the Shared Collection approach (predicated on libraries ceding ownership of materials in perpetuity), the business model for CARM2 offered libraries a long-term licence to an allocation of shelving space on a per linear metre basis. The project was funded by a combination of external financing and pre-payments by Melbourne, Monash and RMIT universities, for which each institution received a proportionate allocation of space at preferential rates over a defined thirty year period. Three blocks of shelving of approximately 15.5 linear kilometres each were constructed, with a fourth block to be constructed as funding allowed. Redundant capacity has been leased by CAVAL on a short to medium term basis to clients from both member and non-member institutions alike, the revenue generated by this contributing to the upkeep of the CARM2 facility and also towards financing for the fourth and final block of shelving. (Jilovsky 2013)

There were several reasons for this change in approach between on the one hand CARM1 and the Shared Collection, and on the other CARM2 and the licensed space model. In essence, these relate to the degree to which individual member libraries could manage and control the future of their holdings housed in offsite storage. Under the terms of the Shared Collection, members ceded ownership of deposited materials in perpetuity, with long-term retention being fundamental to the purpose of the collection. However, this not only commits the library to supporting and maintaining this collection indefinitely, by definition it offers no provision for the membership individually or collectively to reduce the size of the holdings or the cost of its maintenance, even as the value of print retention becomes less apparent. On the other hand, the CARM2 model offers member libraries the ability to take up an allocation of space for the storage of their own materials for a defined period of 30 years, and the flexibility to manage, expand or reduce these holdings as suits their needs and priorities, without obligations to the membership as a whole. (Jilovsky 2013a)

This issue manifested itself in different ways. For example, by ceding ownership of materials entering the Shared Collection, some member libraries noted that this resulted in the writing down of the asset value of their print collections, and that at an institutional level this was not desirable for its negative effect on the financial status of the institution as a whole. Consequently, member libraries with major research holdings became unwilling to commit more of their collections to a shared model which involved loss of ownership. Ceding ownership was also perceived as an issue as it negatively affected metrics concerning library holdings, which at the time of making decisions about CARM2 were still important to assessing the value and status of the library. With the increased availability and take-up of digital resources in the subsequent decade this has become less of an issue, although the growth of digital access has served to reinforce among member libraries the need to exercise control and flexibility in the management of their remaining print collections. (Jilovsky & Genoni, 2013)

Whatever the reason, CARM2 signalled a significant shift conceptually from the thinking which drove the original Shared Collection to a model where libraries share the space rather than the collection itself. Aside from issues of asset value, the CARM2 model enabled libraries to maintain ownership and control of their own collections, offering them flexibility in the length of time materials could be stored offsite, the right (if they chose to exercise it) of withdrawing items or whole formed collections from CAVAL storage and back to the library or disposal, and the ability to house collections which suited the way they wished to manage offsite collections long term, shelving materials in low density "spine out" array, or in high-density packing trays. (Wright, Jilovsky & Anderson, 2012)

The CARM2 model was different also in that it was not viewed solely as a member-oriented exercise, as had been the case with CARM1. Instead, recognizing that maintaining and expanding the facility depended on additional storage revenues, almost one block of shelving as well as redundant floor space has been set aside for CAVAL to lease to members and non-members alike. This has enabled CAVAL to engage a range of library customers from the membership and other academic and special libraries, but to also lease space to museums and galleries in need of environmentally controlled storage space. This has helped in generating revenues to maintain the facility, pending the take up of the space by library clients.

In moving from a shared collection to a shared storage approach, however, what has been lost is the collaborative ability to de-duplicate collections prior to transferring them to offsite storage. The three libraries with major holdings in CARM2 have not attempted to undertake any overlap studies, nor come to an agreement to preserve all or part of their offsite collections in a collective way, for example by committing to a joint storage approach so that savings of space and therefore of cost could be generated. As under the CARM2 model there is no guarantee that the library will retain these holdings long-term, there is also little potential for collaborative enterprise where, for example, other participating libraries could de-duplicate and dispose of collections on the assurance that another library has committed to its retention. In effect, the only collaborative aspect to the CARM2 enterprise is to contribute funding to an offsite storage facility managed by CAVAL.

The Completion of CARM2

The nett effect of this for these libraries and by default for CAVAL, is that the CARM2 facility has filled at a faster rate than the Shared Collection, effectively taking a quarter of the time to fill almost three times the space. An audit of collection space conducted at the end of 2015 revealed that the Shared Collection after twenty years of operations was at 82% capacity, while two of three capital partners in the CARM2 storage facility had effectively consumed their licensed space, and a third (which has opted for re-processing of its collection to high-density storage) was at 65% capacity.

The CAVAL leased space – owing to the decanting of a significant member formed collection during major building works – had also moved rapidly in 2015 from a fill rate of approximately 27% of capacity to 72% in the space of a month, revealing how susceptible CARM2 is to fluctuations from collections being added or removed. The audit also revealed over 20 different customers for leased space in CARM2, only two others of which were member libraries.

The growth in the take-off up of CARM2 space has triggered the planning and construction of a final stage of shelving in the CARM2 facility. Under the original building plan, three blocks of shelving were constructed from the available funds, with the fourth to follow in ten years' time, when it was anticipated that leased storage revenues would be sufficient to fund the final block. The three capital partners will receive additional allocations of space in the new block, in return for their original pre-allocation of maintenance fees. When available in mid-2018, not only will commitments to capital partners be fulfilled, but additional storage pre-paid by one partner library will also be set aside. Consequently, of a structure of approximately 7000 linear metres, approximately only 1300 linear metres will remain for leasing to new customers.

While this figure may fluctuate according to currently occupied leased space being released, what it does signal overall is that the CAVAL membership needs to consider whether there is demand for offsite storage facilities beyond the two CARM facilities, and if so what form a new facility should take.

The Future of the Shared Collection

The first step for CAVAL in determining future print management strategies is to review the different models of collection storage it has developed so far, and to assess the continuing relevance of its print repositories to current and future member needs and priorities. With the Shared Collection in particular, the CAVAL membership has made a commitment to the permanent retention of the collection, reinforced by their investment over a 20 year period in buildings, equipment and personnel to store the collection, make it accessible and preserve it for future use. However, the Shared Collection was conceived at a time when the World Wide Web was in its infancy, electronic journals and databases were only gradually exerting an influence on library acquisition models, there was no mass-digitising of print collections and as yet no practical considerations of e-books displacing and disrupting print publishing. Together with the continuing trend to digital over print in the acquisition and use of resources, does the concept of a print repository based on shared ownership in perpetuity of a resource still make sense?

To date, there has been little research into the composition of the Shared Collection, its usage and its present and future value as a research resource. (Wright, Jilovsky & Anderson, 2012) Without a deliberate collection development policy of its own, the Shared Collection is largely a reflection of the collection policies of its membership, and as a result the collection has been accused of lacking a focus from time to time. However, there are guiding principles in place which have exerted some control over the quality of the resources entering the collection, including the imputed value of materials for research. The effect of these guidelines in practice has been to limit the number of textbooks and similar materials entering the collection, and to encourage libraries to consider the long-term usefulness of materials when making collection relegation decisions. Thus it may be that the collection represents a high standard of scholarship despite the manner in which it has been compiled. Testing this is key to determining the future of the Shared Collection, not only in terms of continuing the current practice of building a genuinely shared collection, but also whether the laissez faire approach to collection development is ultimately sustainable, or some element of active purposeful collection development should be introduced.

The Shared Collection also affords a range of benefits to its immediate membership. The first of these is the opportunity to commit lesser used materials to the collection as an alternative to either retention in the library or disposal altogether. Not only is the cost of offsite shelving per volume significantly cheaper than volumes stored on-site in a library, it also provides members with the opportunity to release and re-purpose floor space in their libraries to provide a greater range of learning environments and other facilities, without the permanent loss of print holdings. In addition, as the collection has built up over time, libraries have been able to check their holdings against the Shared Collection and make decisions with confidence concerning the outright disposal of their copies. Earlier studies (Genoni and Varga 2009, Genoni and Wright 2010) pointed to the untapped potential for the rationalising of print collections in Australian academic libraries, and sample analyses conducted between the CARM Shared Collection and some member libraries (Genoni and Wright 2011) suggest that even after 15 years of relegating materials there was still a moderate degree of overlap between holdings. This has never been tested over the full CAVAL membership and their remaining print monograph and serial holdings, and a comprehensive overlap study may demonstrate that there is a yet to be fully exploited opportunity for members to de-duplicate their own collections. However, against this can be posed the question of whether the Shared Collection continues to remain relevant in the context of increased digital availability of research materials. If a digital version of an item is accessible, is the retention of a last copy print version necessary, and can the expense of its long-term retention and preservation be justified?

Up until the present, the Shared Collection has been created for the immediate needs of the CAVAL membership, and its contents reflect the collection policies of each of its member libraries. As a result, it has developed in isolation from collection development practices elsewhere in Australia, and its relevance at a national scale has never been adequately explored. However, it is clear that many libraries outside of the membership group have also based collection retention or disposal decisions on the permanent availability of items in the Shared Collection, and thus it has by default acquired a national significance. Assessing the value of the collection to CAVAL membership also offers an opportunity to look at its function nationally, and to explore its degree of uniqueness as a national resource.

At this point the CAVAL Shared Collection is only in its first 20 years of what is envisaged to be a commitment to print storage and preservation lasting possibly hundreds of years. While it may have a value as a research resource at present, what factors will determine its value in the future, and will it emerge that such a long time commitment is both sustainable and ultimately necessary? As the Shared Collection enters its third decade, exploring in depth these issues of the continued value and relevance of the collection will guide CAVAL's future directions in the storage of print on behalf of its members, and inform the nature and practice of print stewardship nationally.

Conclusion

In a little over 20 years CAVAL has successfully established two quite different types of print repository. The CARM1 Shared Collection has been designed for truly long-term print storage, with shelving and environmental controls, as well as the policies surrounding CAVAL ownership and inter-filing of materials, purposed to the guaranteed preservation and availability of its contents for many decades if not centuries into the future. The CARM2 licensed space, on the other hand, is intended for the short to medium term retention of materials and offers flexibility without the collaborative potential of central ownership and permanent retention. In building two types of repository, it is a strength of CAVAL that it has responded to the changing priorities of its membership, offering them choices in the future management of their print collections. At a point where it is appropriate and timely to review the value of its print repositories, CAVAL can draw on the experience of developing both approaches to inform and guide its future storage strategies.

References

Genoni, P. and Varga, E. 2009. 'Assessing the Potential for a National Print Repository: results of an Australian overlap study.', *College and Research Libraries*, 70 (6), 555–567.

Genoni, P. and Wright, J. 2010. 'Assessing the collective wealth of Australian research libraries: measuring overlap using WorldCat Collection Analysis.', *The Australian Library Journal*, 59 (4), 197–207.

Genoni, P. and Wright, J. 2011. 'Australia's National Research Collection: overlap, uniqueness and distribution', *Australian Academic & Research Libraries*, 42 (3) 162–178.

Jilovsky, C. 2013. 'The CARM Centre: the creation, revelation and evolution of a print repository', *Australian Academic and Research Libraries*, 44 (2), 113–124.

Jilovsky, C. 2013a. 'The CARM2 Print Repository: from planning to operations', Library Management, 34 (4/5), 281–289.

Jilovsky C. and Genoni, P. 2014. 'Shared collections to shared storage: the CARM1 and CARM2 print repositories', *Library Management*, 35 (1/2), 2–14.

Wright J., Jilovsky C. and Anderson C. 2012. 'The story of a last copy repository in Australia: the CARM Centre stage 2 development', *Collection Management*, 37 (34), 271–293.

Jarmo Saarti

10 Collection policies for the post-digital era of academic publishing – future scenarios for the academic libraries

Throughout their long history, the basic role of the academic libraries has been to ensure open access to scholarly publications in a long-time perspective. This task has remained the same from the very beginning, when unique manuscripts were copied manually, through the collecting of printed resources to the current days of providing and ensuring access to various types of digital and analogue resources.

The advent of digital documents and the creation of digital networks started to change the paradigm of the academic publishing and academic work in whole. The digitization of the scholarly work has even started to challenge the possibility of the academic library net-working and resource sharing between the libraries and their patrons. This avenue has now started to look like a cul-de-sac and we have seen a lot of discussion and even counter actions of the future of open academic achievements (e.g. Beall (2013, 596) sees the open access as denying the freedom of the press).

The present information environment that has forgotten its history is starting to be a barrier to serious academic work. Thus, there is a need for rethinking the collection policies of the academic libraries for the post-digital era. The recent discussion about open science has emphasized the need to ensure the long-time management and preservation of the born-digital materials. And the need for the access to the less used printed resources has not disappeared.

Today, openness and transparency are crucial to the development of research: we have already seen promising results emerging from data mining and other digital techniques that surpass the abilities of the human mind to handle huge masses of digital data. This poses new challenges for academic libraries and their leaders as well as demands for new services. First, it will be essential to invent a new business model for scholarly publishing. It must be recognized that publishing incurs costs that must be covered, especially in the digital environment where long-time preservation of data seems to be a growing, albeit largely unpredictable, cost. And at the same time one needs efficient policies and practices for the printed resources. This paper will analyse the possible solutions for these challenges, the academic libraries are facing presently and in the future.

https://doi.org/10.1515/9783110535372-010

From printed to digital publishing

The printed era of scientific publishing has lasted a couple of hundred years. During this time the structures, practices and traditions of the scientific publishing were created. This includes the genres and their structures – most important one's being scientific monograph and scientific article. Also, the ways how these types of documents are structured were invented and formulated during this historical process.

In addition, the publication process including ways of ensuring the quality and especially the scientific value of each document were modulated. This meant also the networks where the printed works were disseminated to the market were created and there the libraries started to have a major role. The collection building and enabling the use and access to the printed resources were of vital importance to the academic community. On the other hand, it enabled the research and studies which is built on the work of the other academics and colleagues.

The other, and at least as important task for the libraries and their collections became the ethical work that is seldom noted: only the collections that are preserved enable the work against unethical practices in the science and only the collections that are opened to the public enable the critical approach to the science and its results. Thus, the libraries have also an important academic role in the academic community.

This paradigm started to change from the 1990's onward when the digital techniques were introduced. These included firstly the change of the dissemination in the scientific journals: the digital use of the journal articles was initiated.

This on the other hand meant, that the paper based journals started to gradually disappear, though this change is still happening. That meant a radical restatement of the libraries' mission: the main part of the collection was outsourced to the third-party actors, i.e. mainly commercial publishers. The libraries did not anymore own the journals and consequently, they were unable to guarantee the long-time preservation and use of the digital files.

Another main trend was the digitization of the older documents. Here both libraries and publishers were active. This again was impetus for the present collection policy thinking where most of the libraries have started to reduce their printed collections and rely on the use of the digital resources. At the same time the building of printed repositories started to flourish all over the world. The collection policies of the printed era, where the idea for every serious academic library was to collect as much printed resources and preserve the collection for future use ended, and were replaced with the idea of academic library as a learning environment or even a living laboratory for inventions and knowledge creation.

At the present one can see the first – not anymore so weak signals – of a change that has started to happen also in the academic knowledge creation. This has been named as the post-digital world where the main change is that the science is being created solely with the digital tools, totally in the digital realm. We have seen the arise of the new digital environments of publishing, the open science policy building and new types of digital networking tools that enable the researchers to disseminate and collect their work in a library like manner (Muhonen & Saarti 2016).

Printed library		
Warehousing	**Digital library**	
Paper management	E-journal supplier	**Post digital library**
Independence	Paper and digital management	
Local	Dependence	E-resource counselor
Storing knowledge	National	Digital management
	Using knowledge	Co-operation
		Global
		Creating knowledge

Figure 10.1: From printed towards post digital library (see also Laitinen & Saarti 2014, 7).

For the libraries, these all realms still exist and it is most likely that they also will be co-existing for the near future (see Fig. 1.). This means that the strategy work and service modeling for the collection policies and collection use will be of utmost importance for the library network. This because this change does not only enable the academic and other library uses for never seeing possibilities (Pozzi & Pigni & Vitari 2014, 3816), but also sets threads and obstacles especially for the open longtail preservation and use of scientific documents.

Challenges and possibilities of the open science for the libraries and repositories

The open science movement started already in 1990's, although the first discussions being more ideological than practical ones (Ilva & Laitinen & Saarti 2016, 13.). The birth of the pay-walled scientific e-publishing, as already mentioned, changed the paradigm of the academic libraries. They outsourced their collections to the publishers and at the same time news types of restrictions to the open access of scientific publishing started to evolve due to the copyright issues in the digital realm.

The policy level discussion about the open access started from the beginning of this millennium when research funders and national policy makers started to set the open access to the publicly funded research as an imperative not only as a wish (see e.g. European Commission 2012). This on the other hand led to a new type of access to the documents: libraries and other actors started to discuss and implement parallel publishing.

Parallel publishing means that commercially published documents are also published in some form openly, via a parallel publishing information system. For the users and for the libraries this means that another type of edition is being published. This means that the long-time preservation of these documents has become an issue, especially when there is speculations and actions in some libraries to collect all the published documents to be preserved, and if possible, also to accessed via these types of information systems.

The most recent phase of the open science is the need and requirement to open research data to the public including open source codes and open methodology to all the educational and research work produced within the academic community to enhance research and learning to all (Kraker & al. 2011, 645). It seems that the libraries are taking these tasks as a part of their collections and services or at least are collaborating in this process of opening the science. This means that a new and massive types of documents will most likely be integrated to the libraries collections and under their management.

Research data can be seen from the point-of-view of collection policy as very heterogenous, needing special care and knowledge and needing special technologies especially when one considers the long-time preservation of it for the future generations (see more e.g. European Commission 2017). And when comparing this to the traditional collection items that the libraries and repositories are used to deal with at the present, one can say that there are a lot of open questions to be answered, not least the economic resources needed in this type of library work.

Figure 2. depicts the already existing and developing new types of scientific documentation that is happening due to the open science policies implemented. One can already see that the open access will be part of the library collection and preservation policies. Its managing is also easier than the other open science elements since it relies on the traditional rules and practices of the scientific publishing.

Open Access Documents	Open Data	Open Science and Learning Environments
Born OA	Data	Born digital research data and documents
Parallel publishing	Methods	Digitized research data and documents
Hybrid publishing	Metadata and linking	Learning resources and materials

Figure 10.2: Open access and collection policies.

Open data and open science environments are still evolving and most likely will be doing that almost chaotically in the future. At the present, all one can say is that these both will be more difficult to manage than the analogue environment simply because they are both technology and discipline dependent, and they will be changing rapidly in the future. On the other hand, from the point of view of libraries and archives task to enable the reuse and referring to the science and its results, the library community must be active in planning the strategies, tools, and standards how this is enabled and done in a sustainable and manageable way.

New roles, new responsibilities, new technologies

Repository building started mainly from the academic library community (Vattulainen 2004, Paul 2012). There the need to preserve and specially to enable the access and use of the lesser used printed documents were in focus. The other main function was to free space from individual libraries where the economic consciousness grew due to the economic crises from the 1990's onwards and when the library space thinking turned towards thinking the premises as a learning environment for the students instead of seeing them primarily as warehouses for the printed collection.

The fast growth of printed resources hastened this: we did not see the end of the paper era but the birth of an era of hybrid scientific publishing and knowledge dissemination where both digital and printed documents and tools were used. The ideology that was prevalent during the 20th century where the aim of the collection policy was to collect all the possible documented resources for one's own institution ended. One can say that the final death stroke was the initiation of digital document delivery and the ever-increasing prices of the digital resources for the academic libraries.

The digital, as already mentioned, set new obstacles and challenges for the libraries. The copyright regulated documents were difficult, if not altogether impossible to e.g. the traditional inter-library loaning (Howard 2014). And the long-time preservation of digital documents was not as easy as it seemed in the 1990's due to the rapid rise of new data-formats and fast evolving technological environment, including the so-called digital ecosystems with different operating environments and their specific technologies.

Library as an archive		
Long tail management	**Library as a broker**	
Digitization of printed culture	E-document supplier	**Library as an innovation hub**
Lesser used resource management	Open-access publishing costs pay point	Digital science platform
		Knowledge management

Figure 10.3: Scenarios and tasks for the post-digital academic libraries.

The figure 3 depicts three possible scenarios for the future academic libraries (see more about scenario work in libraries O'Connor & Lai-chong Au 2009). These are all conceptual possibilities, in practice these of course overlap each other. Thus, every library must make its own strategical decisions, especially when the scarcity of financial resources must be considered. There also is a need for policies of the division of labor at all the levels: globally, nationally and locally.

The most traditional task of the library – acting as an archive – is not going to perish, although there has been a lot of discussion about the possibilities of digital technologies. At the present there definitely is going on a shift from the traditional printed library towards, maybe an entirely, digitalized library, both from the point-of-view of collections and how the services are provided.

The archival role of the libraries consists of three main tasks that are: the long-tail management of documents, digitization of printed culture and the management of the lesser used resources. It seems that the role of the printed repositories will continue growing. This because the human kind still produces vast amounts of printed books. The major use of both old and new printed resources will mostly be quite modest but especially within the academic community essential. Repositories provide a cost-effective tool for this kind of use. The need here is to start to implement a global policy for the repositories and what and where are to be saved for the future use.

Digitization can be seen here as a two-fold task. On the other hand, it provides new tools for the dissemination of lesser used printed resources – both on-demand-digitization as digitization as a permanent solution – on the other digitization of the publishing culture gives enormous challenges for the library and archive community: how to ensure the long-time preservation of all the digital born documents for the future research use. This seems to be mission impossible if the library community does not learn from the archival community: one must make choices and decisions on what is relevant to be preserved; and one must preserve collections, not individual documents.

The broker role for the libraries was born during the 1990's and has been developing since. It has meant for the libraries a passive role and especially the pay-walled restrictions for the use of digital documents has even started to hinder the actions of the libraries in the long-time management and dissemination of documents and academics in their search for references. This has also meant that the networked peer-to-peer dissemination of documents and tools for that have emerged in the internet (Muhonen & Saarti 2016). The most recent development here is the role of the open-access publishing fees covering in some academic institutions, which means that the costs of the scientific publishing are always to be paid somehow and usually the libraries have a role in it.

This situation needs to be solved and it needs new types of business models for the digital academic world. The long-time preservation of digital documents must be ensured in an open way that enables the use of these resources. In addition, the emerging digital tools for data mining type of research, sets the need for enabling the academics to utilize the digital data as a research object: this means that no publisher or library must be able to set restrictions to this kind of research use from selfish economic interests.

The most recent within the academic libraries have their development toward so-called innovation hubs or centers. One can see the first steps toward this during the 1990's when the libraries as learning centers movement started to evolve (Learning Centres Research Team 2014). The challenges in maintaining both large printed and digital collections, the development of the printed resource repositories and not forgetting the economic downturns have made the libraries to start to rethink their policies concerning the library premises.

But one can already see that this has only been the very beginning of the almost paradigmatic change in the role of the academic library that is happening. The post-digital world that is not about digitizing the analog academic work but creating science in an environment that utilizes social digital tools in all the phases of the academic life has started to evolve.

For the libraries, this means a new opportunity to give their expertise to the academic community in the networks that are being built. Especially there is a need for the knowledge management and digital platforms for the scientific work. It is most likely that this will be a joint effort for all the actors involved in the academic work and the dissemination of its results. What the libraries should offer is especially their knowledge of metadata and collection management which both are crucial for the science and its ethos.

Conclusions

The end of the printed era has been predicted from the very beginning of the digital era. All that one can say at the present is, quoting loosely Mark Twain, that the report of the printed book's death has been an exaggeration. The Telegraph wrote in 13th May 2016: "Books are back: printed book sales rise for first time in four years as ebooks suffer decline". On the other hand, the use of academic journals and their dissemination has been changed from printed to digital in a couple of decades.

One can thus predict that the hybrid co-existence of printed and digital will last at least some decades although the major academic use of documented science will be in the digital format. This since reading books needs time and printed book still is a good interface to longer texts and entireties. The printing technology is also developing rapidly and printing a book has never been as easy as it is at the present. Thus, the bibliographic control, including metadata management and collection building becomes increasingly challenging for the libraries and needs co-operation and division of labor. Here the role of the central repositories for the printed resources and their networking is of utmost importance. There also is a need for lobbying the decision makers for more enabling legislation for the academic community document sharing and use.

At the present, it seems that the resource allocation for the academic institutions and especially to the libraries is challenging. We have seen several economic downturns during the past decades where the budget cutbacks have influenced the collection policies. In practice, this has meant resource re-allocation from the (collection) premises towards other uses (Juntunen & Muhonen & Nygrén & Saarti 2013). Here the centralized repositories have been able to help the libraries also economically and at the same time been able to enhance their service processes (Saarti 2005).

The biggest challenge for the libraries is the emerging e-science. This means new types of services for the academic community and even might mean a change of the role, or at least severe identity rebuilding work for the academic libraries. The emerging digitally perceptive generation of students and academics can already utilize digital tools in disseminating their papers, making their reference databases, and creating metadata for their work, i.e. they have started to act like librarians in managing their academic work.

For the libraries, this can either be a great possibility to start to educate and implement the long tradition of library practices and philosophies to the academic actors; or the library community can complain about the amateurs who are not acting properly and should stay on their own deck. The latter, of course, would mean the end of the academic librarianship or at least it would change the institution to a museum.

The post-digital world of academic work, and academic librarianship, is about networking and use of social digital technologies. This environment changes rapidly, is about making and creating innovation together. This environment breaks down hierarchies, and it values knowledge, ability, and expertise.

But it also needs leadership, because it is quite short-sighted. The core values of academic librarianship, preserving the past knowledge for the future and opening science and its achievements to the public, are becoming even more important than ever in our society that differentiates and where people are becoming unsocial despite the networking technologies available. The libraries have been acting throughout the history as creators of civic societies, this task has not disappeared.

The most invigorating aspect of the recent development of the e-science are the possibilities it is creating in opening science and its result to all humankind; and the new possibilities it is offering for conducting the research when artificial intelligence can be combined with the human intelligence in making new discoveries and managing the great challenges facing the human kind soon. Academic libraries, their collections and their expertise must be part of this evolution.

References

European Commission. 2017. H2020 programme guidelines to the rules on Open Access to scientific publications and open access to research data in Horizon 2020. European Commission, Bruxelles. http://ec.europa.eu/research/participants/data/ref/h2020/grants_manual/hi/oa_pilot/h2020-hi-oa-pilot-guide_en.pdf. [Last visited 8.5.2017.]

Beall, Jeffrey. 2013. The open-access movement is not really about open access. tripleC 11(2):589–597. http://triplec.at/index.php/tripleC/article/view/525/514.

European Commission. 2012. Communication from the Commission to the European parliament, the Council, the European economic and social committee and the Committee of the regions: towards better access to scientific information: boosting the benefits of public investments in research. EU, Brussels. http://ec.europa.eu/research/science-society/document_library/pdf_06/era-communication-towards-better-access-to-scientific-information_en.pdf. [Last visited 14.4.2017.]

Howard, Jennifer. 2014. Library consortium tests interlibrary loans of e-books. Chronicle of higher education, February 17, 2014. http://www.chronicle.com/article/Library-Consortium-Tests/144743. [Last visited 14.4.2017.]

Ilva, Jyrki & Laitinen, Markku & Saarti, Jarmo. 2016. The costs of open and closed access: using the Finnish research output as an example. LIBER Quarterly, 26(1):13–27. DOI: http://doi.org/10.18352/lq.10137. [Last visited 14.4.2017.]

Juntunen, Arja & Muhonen, Ari & Nygrén, Ulla & Saarti, Jarmo. 2013. Reinventing the academic library and its mission: service design in three merged Finnish libraries. In: Mergers and alliances: the wider view: Advances in librarianship, vol. 36:225–246. Ed. by Anne Woodsworth & W. David Penniman. Bingley, Emerald.

Kraker, Peter & Leony, Derick & Reinhardt, Wolfgang & Beham, Günter. 2011. The case for an open science in technology enhanced learning. International journal of technology enhanced learning, 3(6):643–654. DOI: 10.1504/IJTEL.2011.045454. [Last visited 14.4.2017.]

Laitinen, Markku & Saarti, Jarmo. 2014. Evidence based service change: remodelling the academic libraries for the post-digital era. Qualitative and Quantitative Methods in Libraries (QQML Journal) 3(3):611–619. Accessed from: http://www.qqml.net/papers/September_2014_Issue/335QQML_Journal_2014_LaitinnenandSaarti_Sept_611-618.pdf. [Last visited 14.4.2017.]

Learning Centres Research Team. 2014. Learning centres research project: trends in learning centres and library developments: 2008–2013. UBC Okanagan campus library, Kelowna. ok-lib.sites.olt.ubc.ca/files/2014/10/LCRT_Report_2014.pdf. [Last visited 14.4.2017.]

Muhonen, Ari & Saarti, Jarmo. 2016. The changing paradigm of document delivery – exploring researchers' peer to peer practices. Interlending & Document Supply 44(2):66–71.

O'Connor, Steve & Lai-chong Au. 2009. Steering a future through scenarios: into the academic library of the future. Journal of Academic Librarianship 35(1): 57–64. https://doi.org/10.1016/j.acalib.2008.11.001. [Last visited 14.4.2017.]

Paul, Shampa. 2012. Institutional repositories: benefits and incentives. International Information & Library Review 44(4): 194–201. http://dx.doi.org/10.1080/10572317.2012.10762932. [Last visited 14.4.2017.]

Pozzi, Giulia & Pigni, Federico & Vitari, Claudio. 2014. Affordance theory in the IS discipline: a review and synthesis of the literature. In: 20th Americas conference on information systems (AMCIS 2014) smart sustainability: the information systems opportunity, Vol. 5. Association for Information Systems (AIS). AIS/ICIS Administrative Office, Atlanta (Georgia). Pp: 3809–3820.

Saarti, Jarmo. 2005. From printed world to a digital environment: the role of the repository libraries in a changing environment. Library management 26(1–2):26–31.

Vattulainen, Pentti. 2004. National repository initiatives in Europe. Library Collections, Acquisitions, & Technical Services 28(1):39–50.

Pentti Vattulainen

11 The evolving model of the National Repository Library of Finland

The National Repository Library was established in 1988 and opened on 1 March 1989. It was meant to be a repository for all libraries – not only academic but also special and public – as the most economical way of storing library materials. Because of the NRL, the need for extra shelf space in libraries throughout the country has decreased and can be more coherently managed. The material in the Repository Library is received from other libraries and becomes the property of the Library. Thus the transferred material could be de-duplicated, which would allow efficient preservation of printed research material.

Before the library was opened there was a longish planning. Everything started from the realisation that almost all university libraries needed expansion for their collection space. They would continue to do so unless alternative solutions were put in place. At the time universities were funded directly by the Ministry of Education. So the Ministry was very interested in getting a solution that would be permanent and inexpensive.

During the decade of 1980s most university libraries reported collection space problems. Their combined acquisitions were about 15,000 linear metres annually, which would require about 3,000 square metres additional space annually. Most of the material was being little used. The amount of less-used material kept on growing at a faster rate than that of the much-used material.

The NRL would be the most economical method of solving collection space problems. It was thought to be a permanent solution and to allow university libraries to become zero-growth libraries. The instructions to libraries were quantitative: they should transfer material which is equivalent to half of their annual acquisitions and discard (de-duplicate) the rest locally.

There were many international models on which the concept of the Repository Library was developed. The business model of Center for Research Libraries in Chicago was not feasible to Finnish environment. Harvard Depository had an advanced shelving system but it was facility for only one institution. IFLA's Universal Availability of Publications programme made a survey on repository plans and models in 1982 (National..., 1982). Also British Library Document Supply Centre was a model for arranging efficient use of library materials.

https://doi.org/10.1515/9783110535372-011

History and development

National Repository Library – the first repository library for research and public libraries in the world is located in Kuopio 400 km north of Helsinki. The building was an old storage facility which could be easily renovated for library purposes. The main reason for choosing Kuopio was the fact that price level both for purchasing and renting was clearly less than in big cities, especially the Helsinki area. The first hall was renovated in 1988 and 1989 and it had 27,450 linear meters of compact shelves. Libraries started to transfer books and periodicals immediately. The catalogue was opened using the library software VTLS, which was used by all university libraries. The database was planned to be a storage level database which allowed users to locate items. The VTLS union catalogue was created later for information retrieval purposes.

Collections in the NRL grew about 4 linear kilometres a year and interlending started soon. New halls were needed quite soon and they were opened 1996. The shelving was again based on compact shelves. This new two storey hall had finally space of 56,277 shelf metres for books and periodicals. The last hall was opened in 2014. The shelves were of DoubleDecker technology. It allowed to use the whole height of the hall (8 metres) in one space. This solution made it possible to have substantially more material on lesser floor square metres. Compact shelves could hold 13 shelf metres/square metre and DoubleDecker 33 metres/square metre. Total storage floor is 7271 square meters and total shelf space is 111,427 linear metres.

The NRL's activities are directed by a Board of Directors whose members are appointed by the Ministry of Education for three years at a time. The Board was established in order to develop interaction between the NRL and other libraries in Finland. This is important, since the library has no framework organisation of its own.

The role of NRL in Finnish Academic and other libraries: societal impact

1 Savings for university libraries: calculative capital, cumulative

Collection space costs of the libraries can be reduced in Finland by utilizing the National Repository Library (NRL) which is directly funded by the government. It serves especially university libraries by receiving and preserving scholarly and other important material from libraries and by offering this material for use efficiently and free of charge. Because of the NRL, the need for extra shelf space in libraries throughout the country is decreased and can be controlled. Libraries get substantial savings by using the services of the NRL.

University libraries have transferred 90 000 shelf metres to the NRL. Space savings in university libraries is minimum 21 000 square metres. Because libraries can also discard (deduplicate) locally material that already is in the repository, the space savings are much bigger. Average annual rental costs for university libraries are 208 euro/square metre. Cumulative savings for university libraries are at least 4,3 million euro between 1989 to 2015.

During the 25-year period from 1989, the university libraries have transferred altogether 20,676 m^2 or 90,000 metres of library materials to the NRL. Using the average annual rental cost for university libraries of 209 € this equals to total cost saving of 4.3 M Euro. Naturally, this calculation is over estimated since the cost estimate of 209 €/m^2 is based on data from the 2010's (information of annual space costs from 1989 was not available).

During the 2010's university libraries have made collection space savings by transferring materials to the NRL,

Table 11.1: Tranfers of materials to NRL, space cost/m^2 and cost savings/year of university libraries.

	2011	2012	2013	2014	2015	Total
Linear m transferred	2 307	4 396	5 089	5 447	3 611	20 850
m^2 transferred	532,79	1 015,24	1 175,29	1 257,97	833,95	4 815,24
Rent (€/m^2)	189,82	205,24	209,55	207,27	225,70	208,66*
Saving / year (€)	101 133	208 367	246 279	260 733	188 225	1 004 738

* The total of average cost/m^2 was calculated using the by m^2 weighted average space rent that equals to the total space subject to a charge.

Table 1 depicts the total cumulated amount of printed materials transferred from university libraries to the NRL during the years 2011–2015. This is about 21.000 shelf-meters.

In a more detailed analysis about the library materials transferred from the university libraries to the NRL in practice signifies calculated capital savings of the university libraries of the time series 2011–2015. This analysis from the years 2011–2015 shows a total cost saving of 1 M Euro during the period of five years which equals to total savings of 201,000 Euro/year in the university libraries. In practice the amount is bigger due to the fact that all the items sent to the NRL did not became integrated to the collections (e.g. duplicates). (see Saarti et al. 2017). These transfers have allowed the university libraries to live within their building fabric and to save their institutions enormous capital savings for buildings which were not extended or built.

The NRL keeps one copy of each title. The NRL de-duplicates material which is already in its holdings. So far 36% of transferred material has been de-duplicated. What is more important for libraries is the fact that they can locally discard all materials which already is in the NRL. Local de-duplication gives possibilities to make even more savings in collection space costs than transferring materials to the NRL.

Many large university libraries have already transferred most of their print journal collections to the NRL and the amount of transferred material has diminished during last few years. There is still, however, a need to transfer large amounts of books and periodicals to get space for new functions in the libraries. The role of the university libraries has been severly affected by digital disruption. Their roles are significantly different from what they were when the NRL was established some twenty five years ago.

In addition to the estimated savings of space, the university libraries have, too, tangibly cut down their spaces especially in their closed collections. This is especially in other university libraries in contrast to the legal deposit libraries that have the law-based duty to store the legal deposits of Finnish literature.

Most university libraries other than the legal deposit libraries have been able to realize big savings in their closed/special collections thanks to material transfers to the National Repository Library.

2 NRL preserves and keeps available important research material (long tail) and acts as a national interlending and delivery centre

Since 1989, libraries have transferred 150 km of books, periodicals, dissertations and music materials to the NRL. After de-duplication there are nearly 100 km in the shelves. Most of it is catalogued and available in the union catalogue 'Melinda'. 'Melinda' is the union catalogue for university, polytechnic and to a greater extent for public libraries. There is also a collection of 500.000 foreign dissertations in alphabetical order.

In the catalogue there are 1 720 000 titles of monographs and 112 050 titles of periodicals. The biggest languages are English, German and Finnish. In the collections there are items in more than 100 languages.

The use of these resources has been growing constantly. Now the use has reached 100 000 requests or renewals a year. The use is still growing.

The material in the collection is not highly used. An analysis showed that only 7% of the book collections have been used during last ten years. Books are typically requested by public libraries (more than 60% of all loans).

Article copies are mostly sent to university and other research libraries. They are mostly English language STM (science, technology, medicine) articles from 2000s and 2010s.

The NRL has been the biggest interlibrary lending library in Finland since late 1990s. Interlending has been generally diminishing in university libraries for a long time. Much of it has moved to the NRL as its collection grew. Now the amount of lending from NRL is as big as interlibrary lending from all university libraries combined.

A new development over last few years been the creation of initiatives for patron initiated requesting. First the NRL started to use the Universal Borrowing module of *Voyager* software. It allows the library card holders of all Voyager software using libraries to make direct orders from the NRL 24/7. The amount of borrowing and article copies requests has been radically growing during last years.

The National Electronic Library has a user interface called 'Finna'. It opens the collections of the NRL to all citizens – not only library users – and they can place orders directly to NRL. This is still under development but should be more streamlined soon. After that the visibility of the collections of the NRL will be on a new level.

Services are fast and free of charge. Article copies are sent immediately as pdf files. Returnables are mailed and should be in the requesting library next day.

A Nordic study from the year 2003 (Vattulainen, 2003) indicated that repository libraries (in this case Finland and Norway) have clearly lower lending costs when compared with university libraries. The fill rate was also very high. Repository libraries have very good future potential to act as efficient interlending and resource sharing centres.

3 NRL creates and updates good quality metadata received from other libraries

The NRL is adding to its own Voyager database 60,000 to 90,000 records on an annual basis. More than half of them are copied from the union catalogue Melinda (Aleph software). After making necessary corrections they are added to local Voyager data base 'Vaari'. The reason for working in two databases is that the union catalogue does not control the holdings and lending.

NRL also produces new records to the union catalogue and it is in fact the biggest information provider to 'Melinda'. Everything that is not yet in the union catalogue must be either copied from other sources or primary catalogued. The tool for communicating with foreign catalogues is BookWhere.

To diminish the cataloguing work in the NRL, the library has given the transferring libraries permission to work in the catalogue of the NRL before they send materials. Thus the records are already in the NRL catalogue and only have to be activated when they arrive.

4 NRL can be used as a tool for collection management in an individual library

In university libraries budgetary cutbacks have an impact on the collections and the collection policies of the libraries. This is especially the case with the acquisition of the growing digital content collections. The rate of print acquisition is falling due to the nature of digital acquisitions and their annual or contract based pricing – requiring growing amounts of funding. Much of the print acquisition must be made with less and less funding. Because of the existence of the NRL, University libraries can trust that all the print material will be available for them wherever and whenever they were originally bought.

The NRL has been involved with the change from centralized national collection policy towards a decentralized collection management and resource sharing co-operation. (Muhonen et al, 2014) This has been a very significant national library development for a small country such as Finland.

International activities

The NRL has been involved with many international initiatives. It is a member of IFLA and Liber. In both organisations it has been active. The NRL established a discussion group on repository libraries which functioned on 1999–2001.

The NRL has memberships in IFLA's Acquisition and Collection Development and Document Delivery and Resource Sharing section. The NRL has been active in both of them.

The NRL has organized Kuopio conference series. This series concentrated not only on repository libraries but on how to guarantee availability of print materials in times when digital materials are spreading to libraries.

These conference have been documented in several issues of Library Management and also in their web site.

Figure 11.1: http://www.varastokirjasto.fi/calendae-of-events.

The latest initiative is EPICo – European Print Initiatives Collaboration. Many European libraries are participating which is making the initiative strong and viable. The website is: http://www.varastokirjasto.fi/epico

Conclusion: how to rate the success

The annual agreement with the ministry indicates that the whole operation of the NRL is well managed. All goals have been achieved. The mission is clear. Societal targets have been met. The savings for libraries are understandable especially for university libraries. The service level has been high: fast, streamlined, free of charge lending.

The feedback from libraries has been very positive. Repository is one of most valued services to libraries from all sectors

Collaboration with libraries has developed into strong and effective partnerships of advantage to all partners. The NRL has created a collection contact person network which is an advisory network for a national collection policy for print materials. Service agreements clearly formulate what libraries can expect from the NRL and libraries can make quality transfers for de-duplicated materials.

The role of the NRL has been important as the journey from centralized national collection policy towards a decentralized collection management and resource sharing co-operation was made (Muhonen et al 2013)

Politics come in to the library world: a Swan song

The problem with government funding is that different governments have agendas of their own. The existing government has a view to reduce the numbers of small government organisations. The NRL is too small to be an independent organisation and it has to be amalgamated with a bigger institution. In this case the bigger institution is the National Library of Finland. Amalgamation might mean that in a few years there would not be any more a repository library. The previous repository library would be joined as a part of the collection services department of the National Library and to cease existing as an independent organisation.

There are several problems with this plan. Firstly, libraries would lose their direct means to have an influence on the development of the repository as there would not be a board – which represent the library sectors – anymore. The management would be arranged in the same way as any department of the National Library. The second problem is that the National Library is part of Helsinki University. The University has some requirements about the location of the repository. It cannot be in Kuopio anymore.

Another requirement is that the existing collections should be weeded before the move to another town. The National Library also has its own fee policy. It needs to charge for document delivery and interlending. This is against the original concept of developing the repository as the long tail of libraries' collections. In the repository the libraries could trust on getting transferred material fast and free of charge for their users. Another issue is possible charges from transfers of material.

Overall, there is a very proud history of achievement in the National Repository Library, its Board of Directors and the management of the facility. There has been a huge achievement which is greatly admired internationally as a model for development in other parts of the world. Consideration of policy changes will need to be closely consulted with the user groups which have been so closely engaged with the development and more importantly the on-going use of this most unique facility. These users have little alternative. International research indicates that the low-use aspects of the collection will be used and so need to be retained. The NRL is a living testament that although much of the world and Finnish content has become digitised, it is clearly holding unique materials which are vital for the country's on-going research, history and development. The print materials in the NRL are unique and a vital partner in the delivery of content to the citizens of Finland.

References

National Repository Plans and Programmes: A comparative study of existing plans and possible models. IFLA International Office for UAP, Wethrby, West Yorkshire, England, 1982. ISBN 0-7123-2001-6

Muhonen, A., Saarti, J. and Vattulainen, P. 2014. From the centralized national collection policy towards a decentralized collection and resource sharing co-operation: Finnish experiences. Library Management, Vol 35, No 1/2, pp 111–121.

Saarti, Jarmo et al, Effects of digitization to the printed collection policies. Library Management 38, No 2/3, 2017. p. 167–174.

Swansong: https://en.wikipedia.org/wiki/Swan_song

Vattulainen, Pentti: Performance of Interlending in Nordic Academic Libraries, Report for NORDINFO Board 22.8.2003. https://www.kirjastot.fi/sites/default/files/content/perform.pdf

Peter Sidorko

12 Repositioning an Institutional Repository to Capture Research and Data

Background

The University of Hong Kong is the oldest academic institution in Hong Kong and is one of eight universities funded centrally by the Universities Grants Committee (UGC) of the Hong Kong Special Administrative Region (HKSAR) of the People's Republic of China (PRC). On July 1, 2017, Hong Kong celebrated 20 years of its return to Mainland China after 155 years as a British Colony. Under the concept of "one country, two systems", Hong Kong libraries, especially academic libraries, find themselves developing policies within what is a mere microcosm of greater China. Collaborative efforts across the border have occurred but have been relatively selective as issues of funding, cultural distinctions, management practices and significant differences in approaches to print versus electronic collection acquisition and management have hindered progress in a larger regional approach to print and digital repositories.

JULAC (The Joint University Librarians Advisory Committee) is the consortial library entity that brings together collaborative activities of the eight libraries of the universities. The sharing of print collections has been a long held custom among the academic libraries of the eight universities. As growing demands for a variety of uses of library spaces continues to impact academic libraries, the JULAC libraries suffered further spatial pressures when in 2012 the eight universities moved from a three year undergraduate curriculum to a four year one, thereby increasing the undergraduate population by around one third for all institutions and placing ever increasing demands on physical infrastructure. A response to these spatial limitations has been the planning for the development of a single copy, shared storage facility for low use print in anticipation of dire space limitations across the 8 libraries and in response to increasing reliance on all things digital at the expense of print. The Joint Universities Research Archive (JURA), a high density, ASRS (automated storage and retrieval system) driven system, was conceived to ameliorate these issues and to forge a new, enhanced spirit of cooperation among JULAC members. While advanced research, detailed designs and administrative structures have been developed, the physical facility is yet to be realised, awaiting final government funding. This delay has led to an interim solution of de-duplication across the 8 institutions ensuring a single

https://doi.org/10.1515/9783110535372-012

copy is retained within Hong Kong and assigning the responsibility for retention, sharing and preservation equitably across the eight.

The eight academic libraries have also worked assertively in collaboratively acquiring electronic resources and the larger of them now hold major electronic collections that by far surpass their print collections in terms of size, making those print collections increasingly obsolete. These electronic collections have been largely complemented by in-house created databases and repositories through a wide array of digitization projects and the creation and advancement of institutional repositories across all of the libraries. As these repositories transform into, or provide supplements to, current research information systems (CRIS), their significance in the research process grows and provides further opportunities for digital acceleration and exploitation, thereby making print collections even further redundant.

Introduction

Higher Education in Hong Kong dates back to 1911[1] when The University of Hong Kong (HKU) was founded. More than fifty years passed before the second university appeared, The Chinese University of Hong Kong, in 1963. Most recently, the Education University of Hong Kong (founded in 1994 as the Hong Kong Institute of Education) was granted university status in May 2016. The quality of higher education in Hong Kong is well accepted and is confirmed through university rankings tables; The QS World University Rankings® 2016–2017 places three in the top 50 while The Times Higher Education World University Rankings, 2016–2017 places three in the top 100. No other region has such a high percentage of its universities ranked so highly.

The eight libraries that form the JULAC consortium face similar issues to their global counterparts; changes in scholarship and scholarly publishing and new resultant forms of resources to manage including research data, big data and open access resources. From 2005 the JULAC Libraries began to individually respond to these and related challenges through the creation of institutional repositories. Originally conceived in most cases as a contribution to the growing open access initiatives, many institutional repositories have evolved into more complex systems.

---

1 In fact The Hong Kong College of Medicine for Chinese was established in 1887 and later formed the Faculty of Medicine of the fledgling university.

LEARNet, a Learning Object Repository

At the University of Hong Kong discussions for creating an institutional repository date back to 2003. At that time, and dating back to 2002, the Library was managing a learning objects (objects that were then defined as "self-contained, reusable learning resources") repository project known as LEARNet and funded by the University Grants Committee and was based at the University of Hong Kong with a management team drawn from all the 8 UGC tertiary institutions in the HKSAR. Based around the Learning Resources Catalogue (LRC³), created at the University of New South Wales, Australia, as an initiative of Universitas 21 (U21) the project developed a set of tools that enabled cross-institutional collaboration in developing and evaluating learning objects.

LEARNet also provided a means for sharing quality educational resources among the 8 UGC tertiary institutions in Hong Kong. LEARNet materials were designed and produced by Hong Kong academics for Hong Kong students in a range of disciplines. It provided a guarantee of relevance, quality and accuracy through a system of peer review and continuous evaluation. In addition to providing a platform for resources to be stored and shared, LEARNet also provided motivation for the sharing of these objects through financial, technical and pedagogical support for materials developers through the allocation of grant funding. Financial motivation for the creation of innovative resources was a welcome initiative and led to the development of numerous objects from simple images to elaborate game-like learning modules. LEARNet was also intended as a community of practice, providing assistance, evaluation and feedback for developers and users of learning objects. The LEARNet project funded the development and revision of more than five hundred separate resources in the fields of Architecture, Art, Biology, Computer Science, Ecology, Education, Engineering, Languages, Law, Mathematics, Medicine, Music and Psychology. These projects were developed both by individuals at different institutions as well as by cross-institutional groups of academics and included objects that were images, movies, diagrams, interactive graphs, Flash simulations, text, exercises and even whole course modules. Despite this innovative approach, the LEARNet project faded with time largely due to the lack of a sharing culture in higher education in Hong Kong at that time. Nonetheless its creation had stimulated discussions based around developing a similar repository for research output and other digital scholarly content created by HKU's faculty and others.

Establishing and Expanding the HKU Institutional Repository

It was similarly recognised that the fate of a HKU institutional repository could easily follow the same path as the LEARNet project as the willingness of authors to contribute, and therefore share, is a significant aspect of populating such a repository. However, it is not the only measure of success. In a 2003 article Clifford Lynch (Lynch, 2003) describes institutional repositories as:

> "... a mature and fully realized institutional repository will contain the intellectual works of faculty and students – both research and teaching materials – and also documentation of the activities of the institution itself in the form of records of events and performance and of the ongoing intellectual life of the institution."

The University's institutional repository, the Scholars Hub, was launched in 2005 using the DSpace platform. The primary motivation for doing this was to contribute to the open access movement and as an experiment to test the possibility of new publishing and dissemination methodologies. Certain trepidation was experienced given the less than enthusiastic response to the LEARNet project. By 2009, over 25,000 full text items were available in open access through the Scholars Hub. This included over 17,000 theses, 4,000 journal articles, and 2,000 conference papers. Considering that approximately 3,000 articles were annually submitted to Scopus by the University's faculty at that time, this could not be considered a runaway success in terms of comprehensively capturing the University's intellectual output.

In November 2009, the HKU Vice-Chancellor at the time, Professor Tsui Lap Chee, signed the Berlin Declaration on Open Access to Knowledge in the Sciences and Humanities (Max-Planck- Gesellschaft, 2003) on behalf of the University, making HKU the first in Asia to sign the declaration. The Berlin Declaration recognises that information (including research data) should be made widely and readily available to society and encourages and advocates open access publication. While this gesture was recognised in the Library and selectively among faculty as a major breakthrough that would contribute to the development of the Scholars Hub, the overall impact of the signing was more symbolic than providing any dramatic uptake and contributions to the Scholars Hub. Nonetheless, interest in the Scholars Hub was incrementally increasing and the notion of sharing research data was also planted for future discussions.

Also in 2009, a strategic decision was made to enhance the Scholars Hub to encompass more aspects of the University faculties' research cycle. Moving from a static collection of publications (mostly articles and theses) to a more dynamic collection of a broader range of resources that complement those existing and future materials deposited. In fact this enhancement was motivated by a new source of University funding made available for "knowledge exchange". The University developed a new strategic plan (The University of Hong Kong, 2009) which noted knowledge exchange as one of its three pillars (the other two being, predictably, research and teaching & learning). Part of that plan stated "We will continue to inculcate in our academic staff members a culture of knowledge sharing with the public. They will be encouraged to share their intellectual knowledge through public and inaugural lectures, media interviews, publications...". Furthermore, an operational priority pursuant to this strategy was "... setting up a database to record knowledge exchange activities in the University and improving communication within and outside the University, we will facilitate dissemination of information and serve as an exchange hub."

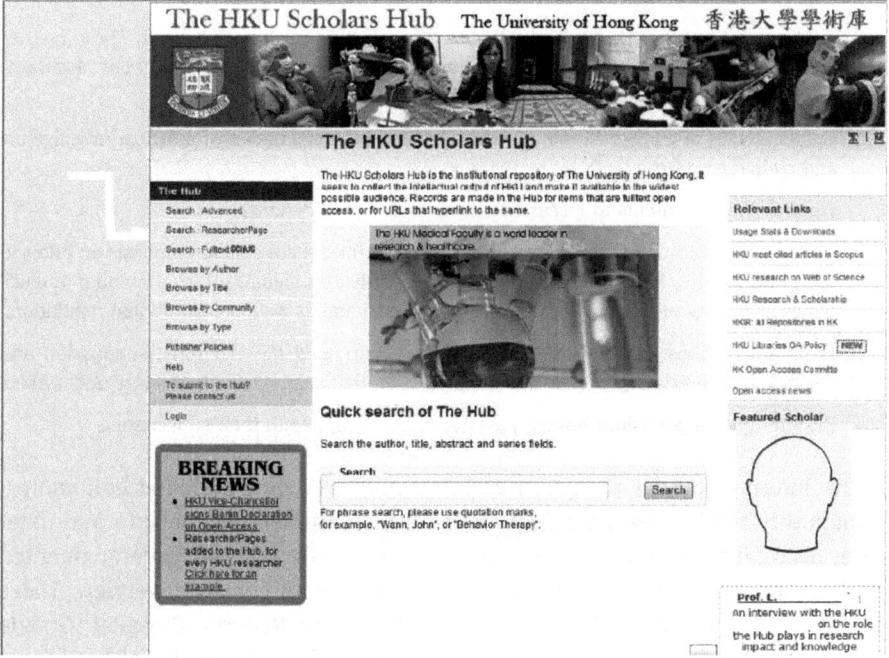

Figure 12.1: The Scholars Hub Entry Page as it appeared in 2009, prior to enhancements.

The obvious choice to pursue this operational priority was the Scholars Hub, but it would require substantial development and enhancement to bring it to the level that would make it the University's database of visible research, a tool to foster opportunities for collaboration and even as a tool for reputation management. A collection of articles and theses would not be sufficient to serve these purposes.

The mechanism by which this was to be achieved was through the contextualising of HKU research, people and expertise through more than just publications. Publications in the form of articles, current theses, books, book chapters and conference papers and presentations had been acquired dating back to 2005 and the processes for capturing these were well entrenched. In order to achieve a more comprehensive and contextualised platform, a dual approach was identified. Firstly, it was recognised that a wide array of relevant information sources were already being collected by a range of administrative and academic units across the university, including the Library. Furthermore these sources were not intended to be ingested and then to remain insular and static but as far as possible they were to be inter-linked in order to facilitate discovery, to enhance visibility and to document and trace the research process.

The internal sources included:

Citation metrics: metrics were obtainable through the Scholars Hub itself. These metrics included researcher page views, document views and downloads. Geographic locations and download numbers were also identified.

Grants: details of grants including funding bodies, amounts, names of principal investigators and co-investigators.

Patents: linking patents to researchers, grants and publications.

Honours and awards: recognising that not all disciplines place similar emphasis on publications and metrics, honours and awards were identified as significant for a number of disciplines as well as means for further promoting individual as well as institutional reputation.

Postgraduate theses: while the University had mandated the electronic submission and deposit of theses dating back to 2001, a project to digitise previous theses was undertaken.

Postgraduate supervision: linking postgraduate research with their supervisors.

Other internal sources identified and ingested over time included editorships, community service, teaching responsibilities, committee membership and datasets. Secondly, the foundational resources internally sourced were augmented with external ones in order to provide a more comprehensive overview. These included: Scopus, Web of Science, Journal Citation Reports, CrossRef, Google Scholar, SciMago and Patents Databases among others. Examples of how these internal and external sources have been incorporated into the Scholars Hub are illustrated in figures 3 and 4.

It became increasingly obvious that what was required for our institutional repository, the Scholars Hub, was for it to evolve into a current research information system (CRIS).

Current Research Information Systems (CRIS)

The enhancements that were identified closely aligned with the evolving concept of a current research information system or CRIS. A CRIS integrates research information that is often maintained and retained in separate systems across an institution. Systems maintained by human resources, finance, student records, grant management, development affairs, media, institutional management units and others. "A CRIS integrates these systems so once information is submitted it enables:

> Efficient capture and exchange of research output information, and monitoring compliance with funder policies;
>
> Automatic updates of researcher, departmental and institutional records;
>
> Showcasing research without the need for manual web page updating" (JISC, 2016).

At HKU this required the Library to play a central coordinating role to facilitate such an integration, as depicted in figure 2.

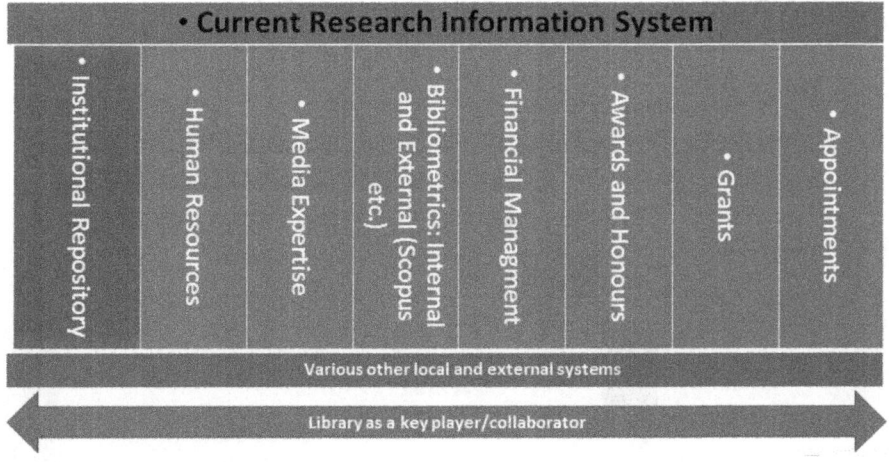

Figure 12.2: Integrating a Range of Disparate Systems into a CRIS.

In order to develop the Scholars Hub to incorporate the identified elements and to contextualize them in order to maximize discovery, visibility and reputation, the Library partnered with the Italian Interuniversity Consortium, Cineca. During these developments Cineca was providing CRIS systems to over 50 Italian institutions and was using DSpace as one of its main solution strategies (Palmer

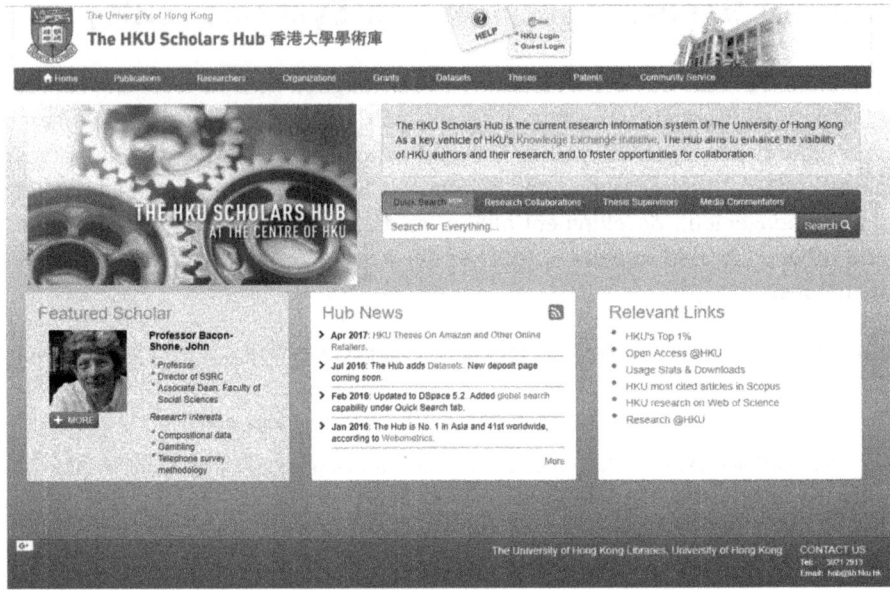

Figure 12.3: The Scholars Hub Entry Page as it appeared in 2017, after enhancements.

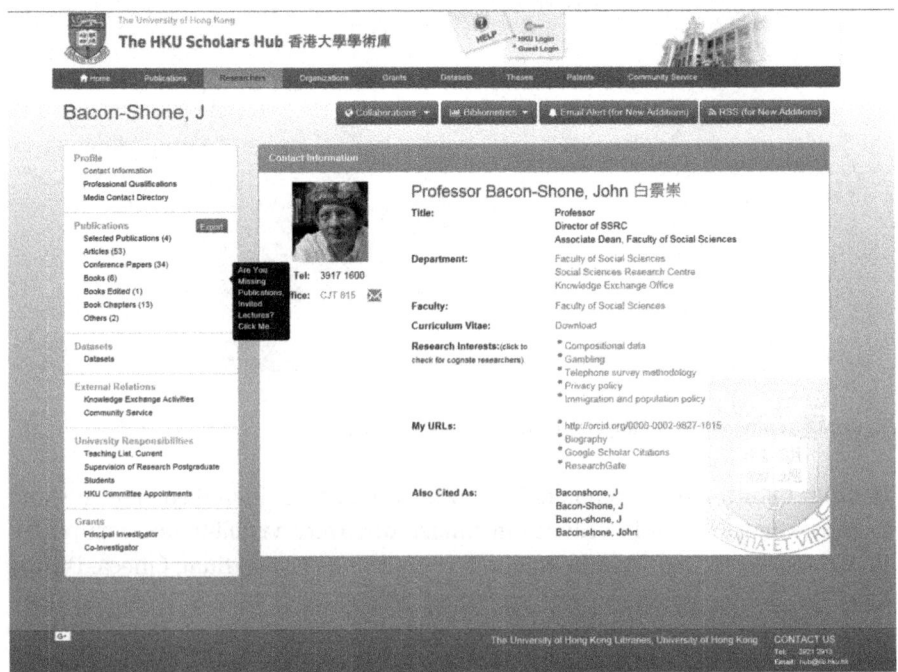

Figure 12.4: The Scholars Hub Researcher Page of the Featured Scholar in Figure 3.

et al, 2014). What evolved from this partnership was the open source DSpace-CRIS. In February 2014, following significant developments of the Scholars Hub, Webometrics the "Ranking Web of Repositories" saw the Hub move from position 169 in the world in July 2013 to number 57 in February 2014, which was the top position in in Asia (Palmer, et al, 2014). A technical description of the development process can be found in Palmer's 2014 article.

Research Data

Recent literature and press surrounding "big data" have led the data discussion. But not all data is big, yet all research data generated from research institutes and universities must be deemed as important. For major research institutions including research universities, all forms of research data, big or otherwise, digital (mostly) or analogue, all serve institutional purpose and these institutions have a responsibility, or at least should have a responsibility, to treat these data appropriately. Firstly, I will discuss the growth in interest in research data and then the practices that research institutions should adopt with respect to their institutionally generated research data using HKU as an example.

There are various means by which research data may be defined. Three different examples of these are provided here to demonstrate three different approaches and purposes for defining research data: (i) specific types of media that contain data; (ii) an inclusive (read vague) institutional requirement definition, and; (iii) a purpose driven definition.

(i) Erway (2013) provides a methodical list of sample types of data as well as a catch all "yet-to-be-identified" category. Promisingly, and relevant to the Scholars Hub as it is an all discipline repository, Erway includes social sciences, ethnographic data and humanities texts in the definition. The data types identified provides us with the challenge to determine if the Scholars Hub can accommodate all of these.

> "... units of information observed, collected, or created during the course of research. This is not limited to scientific data; it includes social science statistical and ethnographic data, humanities texts, or any other data used or produced in the course of academic research, whether it takes the form of text, numbers, image, audio, video, models, analytic code or some yet-to-be-identified data type."

(ii) For institutions with the responsibility to manage research data, ANDS (ANDS, 2017), the Australian National Data Service, defines research data inclusively as:

"... all data which is created by researchers in the course of their work, and for which the institution has a curatorial responsibility for at least as long as the Code and relevant archives/record keeping acts require, and

third-party data which may have originated within the institution or come from elsewhere."

(iii) The United States Federal Government Circular (United States, 1999?) with the subject "Uniform Administrative Requirements for Grants and Agreements With Institutions of Higher Education, Hospitals, and Other Non-Profit Organizations" provides a definition that is purpose driven and thereby is necessarily vague:

"Research data is defined as the recorded factual material commonly accepted in the scientific community as necessary to *validate research findings* (emphasis added)."

Why research data?

I would propose that there are 5 fundamental reasons why research data has developed in significance and why research institutions, universities and grant funding bodies are paying greater attention to the management of institutionally created research data.

1 Growth in research output

Pressure on university faculty to publish as one of a number of means of achieving tenure, has led to an ever growing number of scholarly journals: commercial, open access, and hybrid versions. The number of publishing options for faculty has never been so abundant. This abundance has fed the desire to publish as well as meeting a growing demand by faculty, especially research faculty. While not all journal research articles (and I use journal articles here as the dominant format chosen by faculty and where the overwhelming majority of research output can be found, but it must also be recognised that monographs, chapters, conference papers, etc. are all included in this growth) require the creation of research data, it is without doubt that the overwhelming majority do generate some data, irrespective of the size or complexity.

2 Competitiveness

Related to growth in research output is the concept of competitiveness. There are two aspects to this concept in terms of research data and attribution to its growth. Firstly, while collaboration in research is increasingly rewarded by institutions as well as funding bodies, there remains a strong competitiveness among researchers be they from the same or different institutions. Such competitiveness, competitiveness for funding, for being first, for solving a conundrum before other experts in the field, all in turn drive research. This represents positive competition that drives research further resulting in advances that benefit society. With more research … well, at this point return to number 1, above.

The second aspect of competitiveness is somewhat less positive, though its outcomes may be positive. The world of the researcher can be cruel and vindictive. Accusations of data manipulation, fabrication and creation do exist. And, while not rampant, such accusations do exist and appear with widespread coverage (at least across the discipline's literature) and can result in the destruction of a prestigious career and the diminution of an institution's reputation. I mention that this may have a positive effect. Anything positive resulting from such a process would be in the form of correcting false research. However, if such accusations are unwarranted, a stigma (right or wrong) remains with the accused. This of course has served to encourage research institutions to ensure that research data that supports/dispels such accusations should be retained in order to validate the research and resolve the matter, in at least some cases, expeditiously.

3 Integrity

Closely aligned with the second aspect of competitiveness noted above is the issue of data integrity. Data retention is a fine start for validating research into the future. However, to ensure the integrity of the data, assuming that what was presented initially for storage carried such integrity, it is essential that retention is secure, preserved and usable into the future in the manner in which it was intended. This involves components of data curation to ensure these aspects are adhered to.

4 Re-usability and sharing

Research is usually expensive, though this varies across disciplines and is also dependent on the nature of the research. As such, it makes quite obvious sense for data that has been generated from one researcher and which may be useful to another researcher to be shared. There are obvious limitations that may apply to making re-use and sharing complicated: confidentiality of personal data; sharing across jurisdictions (funding bodies etc.); sharing among competitive institutions; the degree of applicability and relevance of the data; the age of the data, and; an inherent possessiveness and unwillingness to share across academia (real or perceived). Irrespective of this, there is increasing pressure placed by funding bodies and research institutions for researchers to make their research data accessible by others, be it globally, nationally, locally, institutionally, or within one's own faculty or department.

5 Commercial benefits

As noted in 4 above, research is typically costly and efficiencies can be gained through sharing of relevant data that saves on time and resources in recreating the same results. At a national level however the benefits of such sharing has the opportunity to advance research and to create significant commercial gain. A 2014 study by the Australian National Data Service (ANDS, 2014) found that the full availability to publicly funded research data had the potential to generate $A5.5 billion per year. Were this to be re-injected into publicly funded research, and the data generated from that research made publicly accessible, a cycle of continuous funding for research that leads to improvements for society and national competitiveness in turn makes governments supportive of national research data sharing.

Research Data at HKU

These 5 factors combined provide librarians in research institutions and universities with an obvious opportunity. At the University of Hong Kong we conducted the Ithaka S+R survey into faculty research in 2014. While the number of respondents were disappointingly low (115), several of the responses alerted us in the Library to a need that had not been met but provided an opportunity for the Library to take a lead. In response to the question "Who manages your data?", 88% of respondents ranked between 8 and 10 the response "when I am in the process of collecting data, media, or images for my research I often organise or manage these data on my own computer or computers". By contrast only 6% of respondents ranked between 8 and 10 the response "my university library manages or organises my data, media, or images on my behalf".

Further, when asked "How valuable would you find each of the following for managing or preserving research data, media, or images?", 69% of respondents ranked between 8 and 10 the response "my university library". Similarly, 68% of respondents ranked between 8 and 10 the response "freely available software".

Several things can be gleaned from the responses to these two questions. Firstly, and not unpredictably, our faculty are overwhelmingly storing their research data on their own computers. In the context of the 5 factors mentioned above, this cannot be recognised as a satisfactory methodology. The limitations of such storage are numerous including the potential loss of data due to hard drive corruption, loss of data when upgrading computers, preservation in terms of future re-usability, the lack of visibility and the low opportunity for sharing to name just a few. Secondly, a significant number of respondents (69%) felt strongly that they would find it valuable if the library managed and preserved their research data, media, or images.

Together these two responses heralded a call for the library to respond. Fortuitously, the University, through its Research Committee, was formulating a policy related to research data management and in April 2015 the Policy on the Management of Research Data and Records was passed by the Senate (The University of Hong Kong, 2014). The reasons for doing so were primarily:

- To meet the need to replicate claimed research results when called upon to do so, and;
- To meet the need to ensure ethical data collection, storage, and if chosen, re-sharing of data.

In general, this policy set out responsibilities for HKU researchers (academics and research postgraduate students), to:

- Perform research data management (RDM) through a data management plan (DMP), and;
- Ensure ongoing custodianship of their data after the completion of the research.

The Policy further described responsibilities of the University to:

- Provide access to services and facilities for the storage, deposit and retention of research data;
- Provide access to training, support and advice in RDM, and;
- Provide resources to operational units charged with provision of these services, facilities, and training.

The policy was to be effective for the 2017 postgraduate student intake and for grant applications by faculty starting in 2018. The Library was chosen to address the bulk of the University's responsibilities. Of significance to this chapter, the task of providing access to services and facilities for the storage, deposit and retention of research data is the most relevant.

Research Data and The Scholars Hub

Although the Scholars Hub had already been used as a current research information system (CRIS) for several years, there was some question as to whether the Hub was the best platform for datasets as well, both functionally and economically. A key consideration was the need for recurring funding to commit to alternate platforms requiring ongoing subscriptions. Several alternative platforms were considered but eventually it was agreed that the Hub was functionally fit for purpose for the storage, deposit and retention of research data, it was also the most economical choice, and the quickest option to implement. This was also considered the ideal solution as we had invested significant technological, financial, and human resources into developing the Scholars Hub into a current research information system which we had envisaged to be a tool that would track the full, or as full as possible, research cycle of our faculty and, to a lesser extent, our research postgraduate students.

A first hurdle in using the Scholars Hub was that, while we had Hub pages for each of our faculty researchers, we did not have Hub pages for research postgraduate students. In 2016 we started to develop and prototype Researcher Pages for research postgraduate students in the Scholars Hub. A system for automatically generating and populating these pages was also developed. Students are now able to highlight their research as developed at HKU as well as listing any achievements, publications or other relevant information related to their studies and research.

Secondly, as the policy for deposit was only to be effective from the 2017 intake of postgraduate students and the 2018 grant applications by faculty, it is conceivable that direct deposit resulting from this policy will not occur until 2018 at the very earliest. Until that time the deposit of research data has been encouraged but not mandated. Procedures, templates as well as online submission, description and upload have been activated on a voluntary basis. Additionally, the Library has been actively identifying datasets that our faculty have deposited in third party repositories such as Figshare and providing the appropriate metadata for these datasets. To date some 400 unique sets of data are now accessible through the Scholars Hub. Records for all 400 datasets provide relevant metadata including title of dataset, author(s), creation date(s), description, citation, subjects (using relevant granting bodies' codes), keywords, DOIs etc. Additionally links to the dataset files themselves are provided where possible, as are links to relevant publications resulting from the research, links to grant information that funded the research, the terms of use i.e. whether and under what conditions the datasets may be re-used and where available links to any publications where the dataset itself has been cited. Image 4 illustrates these features.

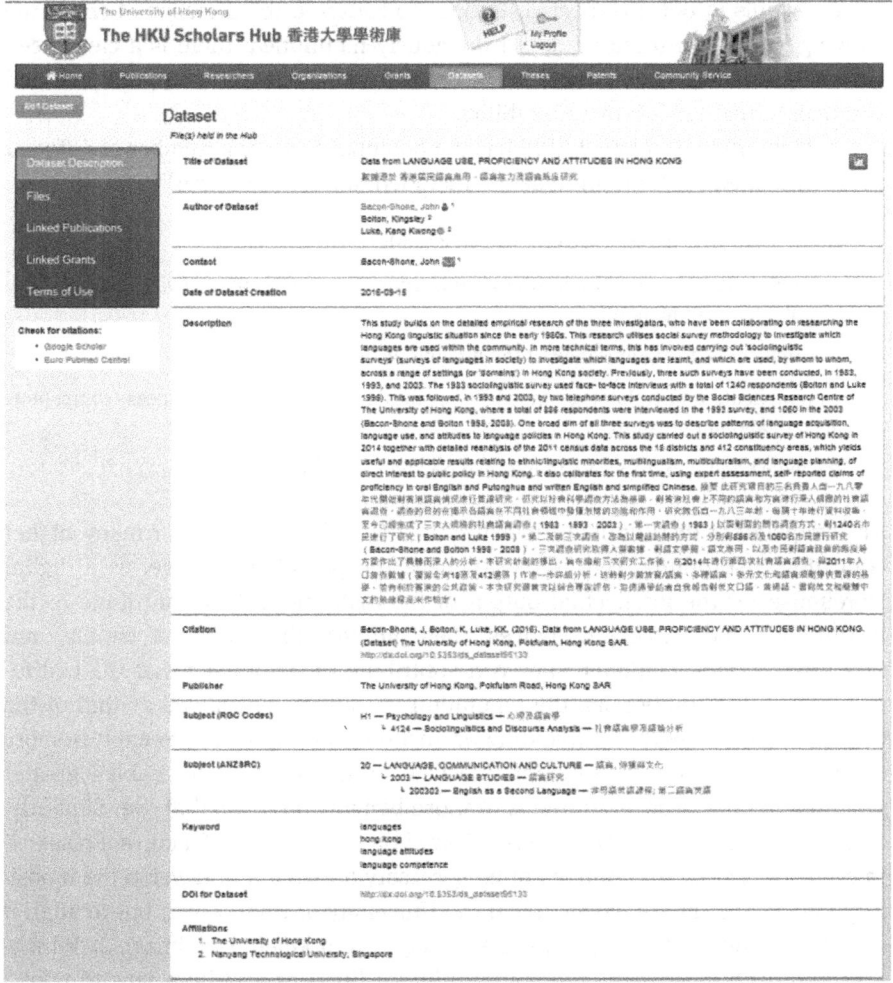

Figure 12.5: A sample dataset page.

Conclusion and Future Directions

The development of CRIS systems in recent years has been significant as research institutions and funding bodies demand greater accountability and efficiency. Elements (Symplectic), Converis (Clarivate) and Pure (Elsevier) are just 3 such systems that have evolved in order to meet this need. DSpace-CRIS, as already mentioned, has been developed from DSpace to better accommodate and document research output in all its forms. The growth in number and popularity of these systems is not unexpected. By just considering the 5 reasons behind the growing interest in research data I previously mentioned, there is a clear need for data plus all the other elements of the research cycle to be properly retained and maintained for future accessibility.

In fact a fully developed CRIS has the potential to serve a number of different needs and stakeholder requirements. Included among these are:

researchers (easy access to relevant information);

research managers and administrators (measurement of research activity and access to comparative information);

research councils (optimisation of the funding process);

entrepreneurs and technology transfer organizations (access to novel ideas, competitors and collaborators), and;

the media and public (access to information and innovations) (Wikipedia, 2017).

An independent institutional repository is a valuable resource for many higher education institutions. They serve, or have the potential to serve, as a digital storehouse for the intellectual output of the institution. They contribute to the institution's open access initiatives, they promote the output of faculty, and to a lesser extent, students. They can contribute to the impact that the institution has on the community, the reputation of individuals as well as that of the organization as a whole. Expanding an institutional repository to capture more elements related to the research lifecycle of the institution enables greater potential to be unleashed in terms of those benefits mentioned above. Similarly, an institutional repository can be considered one component of a current research information system and it may not be necessary to expand or develop the repository into a CRIS, as we have done at the University of Hong Kong, but to align it with other campus systems to form an integral component (see image 2). Whichever approach is adopted, the opportunity for libraries and librarians to take a leading role, having gained experience in developing institutional repositories, provides both a challenge and a major opportunity to work across a campus with disparate systems in order to achieve the benefits promised through a current research information system.

While the full potential for institutional repositories and current research information systems remain significant, the previously mentioned, Joint Universities Research Archive (JURA), a high density, ASRS (automated storage and retrieval system) driven system, continues as a high priority for the eight university libraries in Hong Kong. This print based repository is of significance, not only as it will serve to free up much needed space in the 8 libraries for other purposes but "... will create the largest single historical archive of western research materials in Asia and will become an unrivalled centre for scholarship and research" (Sidorko and Lee, 2014). Hong Kong's unique geopolitical position places extra significance on this collection. As a microcosm of international best practice in higher education, Hong Kong holds a responsibilty for the stewardship of its legacy print collections as well as for its digital repositories. The future challenges will centre on the ability to seamlessly integrate the two and to exploit them for all of their stated purposes.

References

ANDS. 2017. *ANDS Guide: What is Research Data*, Australian National Data Service, viewed 26 August, 2017 from http://www.ands.org.au/_data/assets/pdf_file/0006/731823/What-is-research-data.pdf.

ANDS. 2014. *Open Research Data Report*, viewed 22 August, 2017, from http://ands.org.au//resource/open-research-data.html.

Erway, R. 2013. *Starting the Conversation: University – wide Research Data Management Policy* (p. 5). Dublin, OH: OCLC Research, viewed August 28, 2017, from https://www.oclc.org/content/dam/research/publications/library/2013/2013-08.pdf.

JISC. 2016. *Manage your research information*, viewed July 30, 2017, from https://www.jisc.ac.uk/guides/manage-your-research-information.

Lynch, C. A. 2003. Institutional repositories: Essential infrastructure for scholarship in the digital age. *ARL: A Bimonthly Report*, no. 226 (February 2003), viewed 31 July 2017, http://old.arl.org/resources/pubs/br/br226/br226ir~print.shtml.

Max-Planck-Gesellschaft, 2003, *Berlin Declaration on Open Access to Knowledge in the Sciences and Humanities*, viewed 30 July, 2017 from https://openaccess.mpg.de/Berlin-Declaration.

Palmer, DT; Bolini, A; Mornati, S; Mennielli, M. 2014. *DSpace-CRIS@HKU: Achieving visibility with a CERIF compliant open source system*. The 12th International Conference on Current Research Information Systems (CRIS 2014), Rome, Italy, 13–15 May 2014. In Procedia Computer Science, 2014, v. 33 p. 118–123, viewed 28 August, 2017 from http://hub.hku.hk/handle/10722/198431.

United States. 1999?. *CIRCULAR A-110 REVISED 11/19/93*, As Further Amended 9/30/99, viewed 23 August, 2017 from https://www.whitehouse.gov/omb/circulars_a110.

The University of Hong Kong. 2009. Strategic Development, 2009–2014, viewed 25 August, 2017 from http://www.sppoweb.hku.hk/sdplan/eng/strategic-themes-for-09-14/.

The University of Hong Kong. 2014. *Policy on the Management of Research Data and Records*, viewed 25 August, 2017 from http://www.rss.hku.hk/integrity/research-data-records-management.

Wikipedia. 2017. Current research information system, *Wikipedia, The Free Encyclopedia*, viewed 28 August, 2017, at https://en.wikipedia.org/w/index.php?title=Current_research_information_system&oldid=795648460.

Jean-Louis Baraggioli

13 Coordinating a National Policy for Shared Conservation

Tools and Methods of Shared Working

The historic mission of CTLes has been the establishment of the book silos, missions traditionally devolved to depository libraries for printed documents. The institution's actions have, however, diversified with the implementation of Decree no. 2014-320 of 10 March 2014, which entrusts the institution with a major role in setting up and monitoring the shared periodical conservation plans (PCPs) which are developed at the national level[1]. This is a very significant development.

The scope of action of the Depository Library is now extended to the national level and has been further enhanced with a new mission. The latter translates into an active, albeit modest, involvement in coordinating the acquisition policies of the CTLes partner institutions. It also has implications for the nature of the collections that CTLes is obliged to accept when it comes to collections which are ceded to it and which constitute its own collections. The institution is now an essential lever in defining the directions taken by its parent ministry in the field of scientific information within the French documentary network. It is in this capacity that it is called upon to coordinate a national policy for the shared preservation of periodicals.

The PCPs co-facilitated by the CTLes make it possible to establish a network of institutions that guarantee the enduring conservation and communication of printed periodicals. The aim is to offer teachers and teacher-researchers a body of sources described in the national tools in a detailed and precise way. Regional networking at a national level should allow for the creation of several reference collections for the same title, while facilitating large-scale thinning operations to free up space.

---

1 Article 2 of Decree no. 2014-320 of 10 March 2014: "The centre shall collect, manage, preserve and communicate books and documents of scientific and heritage interest which are entrusted to its keep by the public institutions under the responsibility of the Minister for Higher Education and in particular by those which are located in the academies of Paris, Créteil and Versailles. The terms and conditions of storage are determined by an agreement between the centre and the institutions. The centre may also set up and manage a collection of its own from the books and documents whose ownership is transferred to it by the institutions. It shall support, as necessary and in accordance with its technical capacities, the institutions concerned for the conservation and physical preservation of their books and documents, primarily in paper form. »

https://doi.org/10.1515/9783110535372-013

From Piloting to Implementation

A structured organisation

Each conservation plan is thematic. The rule followed today is to put each title in a single plan. There cannot be the same title in several plans. To the extent that the number of PCPs is still limited[2], choices are not difficult to make. The aim is to constitute one or more complete collections of the same title which will be preserved in a permanent way within libraries called conservation centres. An institution can be a conservation centre for one title or several thousand titles. The quality of the conservation centre is assessed title by title.

The idea is, however, to limit the number of complete collections within the network and to allow each partner library to continue or interrupt subscriptions for the titles concerned.

For the institutions, as for CTLes, adhering to a conservation plan requires work to completely renew the condition of collections, both in stores and in SUDOC. It is important that the catalogue is an exact reflection of the material collections preserved in the establishments. In-store inventory checking is the first job on the ground and is the beginning of a logic of empowering each participant. This is part of a process of collective cohesion within the network. Carrying out the inventory check, which will make it possible to measure the involvement of the libraries in a PCP, is undoubtedly the first indicator of their commitment.

Concurrently, as soon as a PCP is launched, CTLes makes available to libraries two management tools, the aim of which is to support and reassure participants in their actions. These tools are as follows:
- The *Periodicals Management Database*, which allows for precise identification, for each title concerned, of the condition of the collection, gaps and conservation centres. This database, fed by SUDOC, facilitates thinning operations[3].
- The *Collaborative Work Platform*, which helps organise and manage the monitoring of transfers of collections between institutions, provide indicators for reorienting the document policy, compile statistics and collect methodology documentation[4].

It goes without saying that to take advantage of the tools, it is necessary to stick to the principles that have been established collectively by a working group

---

2 As of 1st March 2016, the PCPs co-facilitated by CTLes cover the following themes: Medicine, Performing Arts, Philosophy, Geography and Urban Planning, Sports Science.

3 http://pcp.docressources.fr/opac/

4 http://floraweb/flora/

composed of directors of university libraries in Ile-de-France, notably based on the rules that were drawn up in 2005 with the implementation of the Medicine PCP.

The principles that govern PCPs are:

- The arrangement covers printed collections, both live titles and dead titles.
- The network consists of reference libraries (conservation centres) and partner libraries.
- The network is led by a scientific co-facilitator (a library centre of excellence for the thematic segment concerned) and a technical co-facilitator (CTLes).
- The collections must be owned by the participating libraries, which may transfer ownership to other members of the network.
- Any conservation centre may revise its position on certain titles and stop carrying them as a conservation centre, provided that the baton can be taken up by another library in the network.
- The conservation centres undertake to guarantee access to the collections they maintain on an enduring basis by participating in interlibrary loan arrangements and/or by welcoming in readers.
- Transfers of collections between institutions are organised by mutual agreement. In the Ile-de-France region, CTLes can offer logistical support by providing a transfer service.
- Thinning is carried out in a concerted manner, after making sure that the documents concerned are not likely to fill gaps in the reference collection or possibly a collection in a partner library.

Each time a new PCP is launched, CTLes intervenes at two separate points. First and foremost, at the launch of the plan, as co-pilot, a privileged partner of the library specialising in the thematic segment that is the subject of the PCP. For these two institutions, this means dividing up the tasks that will make the PCP efficient and attractive for other libraries.

As a general rule, defining the corpus is beyond the expertise of CTLes and is the first task that the library supporting the plan has to carry out in its capacity as scientific referent. At this decisive moment, which marks the launch of the shared conservation plan, CTLes is called upon to intervene at several levels for training in the tools available to the community: The *Periodicals Management Database* and the *Collaborative Work Platform*.

Intervention levels in the *Periodicals Management Database*

Once the list of titles is finished, CTLes intervenes with the ABES so that the records and the condition of collections of the selected titles are placed in the *Periodicals Management Database.*

CTLes must train the agents who will have to intervene in this database to indicate in particular if their establishment is a conservation centre.

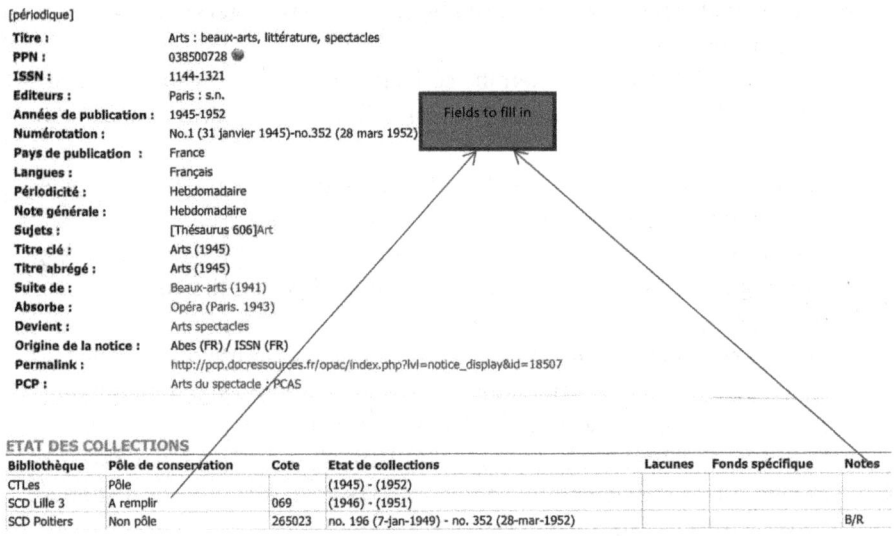

Figure 13.1

For CTLes, it is about explaining the structure and rules that should make it possible to complete the information relating to each title. Data concerning the state of the collection and, where applicable, any gaps, are entered in the SUDOC and imported into the database during regular updates. The possibility of a real-time update of the database is currently under investigation.

Intervention levels in the *Collaborative Work Platform*

The operations of inventory checking, collection status correction and reporting of gaps must theoretically be carried out on all titles for which a library is located in the *Periodicals Management Database,* in order to facilitate subsequent work on "*donation proposals*" and requests for filling in gaps which we call "*wanted notices*". It is imperative that these operations are carried out systematically for the titles for which an institution wishes to be a conservation centre.

The *Collaborative Work Platform* is the tool for making *"donation proposals"* and launching *"wanted notices"*.

CTLes must also provide all the libraries participating in a PCP with the necessary training in the use of this tool. It must also ensure the formalisation of the various forms and ensure that the different partners respond to the *"donation proposals"* and *"wanted notices"* within a reasonable timeframe.

Libraries wishing to get rid of collections integrated within the plan must first ensure that the publications or volumes to be scrapped are not likely to complement the collections of the corresponding conservation centre(s).

A *"donation proposal"* should therefore be placed on the *Collaborative Work Platform*.

The form template, shown below, is available in the *"Methodological Tools"* folder.

PPN	ISSN	Titre de périodique	Etat de collection proposé	Relié (R) ou non relié (NR)	Etat physique - bon (B) / correct(C) / mauvais (M)	Etablissement(s) PCMed localisé(s)	Etablissement(s) PCMed pôle(s)	Observations
03921921 6	0001-7817	Actualités odonto-stomatologiques (liste 22)	vol.54 (2000) - vol.63, n°271 (2015)	NR	B	BIU Santé pôle Médecine CTLes Paris 5 - Montrouge Paris 6 - Dechaume Paris 7 - Garancière	BIU Santé pôle Médecine Paris 5 - Montrouge	
03886220 5	0002-8703	American Heart journal (liste 5)	vol. 135 (1998) - vol.171, n°2 (2016) Lacunes : vol.146, n°5 Suppl. (nov-2004) ; vol.149, n°4 Suppl. (avr-2005) ; vol.153, n°4 Suppl. (avr-2007) ; vol.155, n°3 (mar-2008) ; vol.15,7 n°6 Suppl. (jun-2009) ; vol.160, n°6 Suppl. (dec-2010) ; vol.165, n°5 (mai-2013)	NR	C : vol 135 (1998) - vol 138 (1999) B : vol. 139 (2000) - 2014	BIU Santé Paris 5 - Necker Paris 6 - Axial-Caroli Paris 6 - Pitié-Salpêtrière Paris 7 - Bichat Paris 11 - Kremlin-Bicêtre Paris 12	BIU Santé pôle médecine	La BANM a arrêté l'abonnement à cette revue.

Figure 13.2

The relevant *"wanted notice"* form allows libraries that so wish to fill their gaps with the collections of other participating libraries.

The form template below is available in the *"Methodological Tools"* folder.

PPN	ISSN	Titre de périodique	Lacunes à combler	Etablissement(s) PCMed. susceptible(s) de combler ces lacunes	Observations
037460668	2022-1355	Congrès des médecins aliénistes et neurologistes de France et des pays de langue française	1897-1898 1900 1906 1908-1909 1914-1919 1921-1922 1926 1937-1955 1957-1958	BIU Santé P6 - Pitié Salpêtrière P12 - Créteil	
039724239	0762-7475	Synapse	n°90 (nov.1992) n°214-217 (avr.-sept. 2005) n°219 (nov. 2005) n°230 (2006) 2007-2008	BIU Santé CTLes P5 - Henri Piéron P11 - Kremlin-Bicêtre P13 - Bobigny	La BANM est pôle de conservation.

Figure 13.3

Thinning operations are carried out by each establishment concerned, and should result in the establishment of a *"disposal slip"*, based on the template available on the shared work platform.

Titre	ISSN	Métrage pilonné (en ml)	Pôle(s) de conservation	Pilon faisant suite à la proposition de don en date du (format jj/mm/aaaa) :	Observations éventuelles
Virology	0042-6822	4,16	BIUS	08/06/2015	
Enzymologia	0013-9424	0,75	BIUS - Pharmacie	08/06/2015	
Endocrinology	0013-7227	8,02	BIUS	04/06/2015	
Biologie médicale	0006-3266	1,24	BIUS	19/06/2015	

Figure 13.4

Transfers of collections, whether managed by CTLes or by another participant, must result in the filing in of a "*transfer slip*" on the *Collaborative Work Platform*, to allow for the production of statistics. The slip must be created based on the template provided for this purpose and available on the platform.

Bordereau de transfert

	Établissement émetteur	Établissement destinataire
Nom	BIUSanté	Bibliothèque de l'Académie nationale de médecine
Adresse	12 rue de l'Ecole de médecine 75006 Paris	16 rue Bonaparte 75272 Paris Cedex 06
Responsable du transfert	Isabelle Peyret	Anaïs Dupuy-Olivier
Téléphone	01 76 53 18 95	01 46 34 88 86
Adresse électronique	isabelle.peyret@biusante.parisdescartes.fr	anais.dupuy-olivier@academie-medecine.fr

Date du transfert: 12/01/2016

			État physique du document				Format			Localisation dans le Sudoc			Mise à jour dans le Sudoc		
Titre du périodique	ISSN	État de collection	relié	non relié	Etat (Bon/Mauvais /Correct)	Métrage estimé (en ml)	in-4°	in-8°	in-16	en totalité	en partie	pas du tout	date de délocalisation	date de localisation (pôle de conservation)	Observations
France médecine	0150-3308	n°62,1976		x		0,001	x			x			14/01/2016		
Journal of audiovisual media in medicine	0140-511X	vol.1 (1978) - vol.3 n°1 (1980) ; vol.11 (1988) - vol.20 (1997)		x		0,21	x			x			14/01/2016		
Philadelphia Hospital reports	1877-7954	vol.6	x			0,03		x		x			14/01/2016		

Figure 13.5

Each stage of the process depends on the previous one and produces effects on the next. CTLes supports its partners step by step and ensures in particular that deadlines for processing lists of titles are respected. Such coordination is necessary because it ensures the coherence of operations and helps develop synergies.

The second intervention takes place at the time of the annual review. Beyond the review, which takes the form of a report drafted jointly by CTLes and the library which is the scientific referent, ie the centre of excellence on the thematic area concerned.

The purpose of this document is to collect numerical data on what has been done during the year and also, prospectively, to set the directions to be taken during the following year. A meeting with all members of the network makes it possible to establish CTLes in its role of PCP coordinator and co-facilitator.

CTLes in its role as coordinator

Participants interact through communication that takes place through a mailing list. Instructions are given both by CTLes and the library that holds the conservation plan (library specialising in the thematic segment). CTLes nevertheless guarantees the execution of the work according to the procedures and specific rules determined collectively with all the participants in the PCP. Finally, CTLes provides the training required to use the tools and guarantees the standardisation of results.

The role of coordinator is decisive for the overall performance of the various PCPs, allowing the implementation of a proper network of relations between the partners based on the unifying role of the tools. It also enables CTLes to act as the sole intermediary with the Bibliographic Agency of Higher Education (ABES) for the remittance of bibliographic records and collection statuses extracted from SUDOC in the *Periodicals Management Database.*

In its role as coordinator, CTLes defines with the ABES the codes for reporting PCPs in SUDOC.

This model for resource coordination in France is an exciting and very carefully thought-through suite of processes.

Extract from the SUDOC relating to a periodical belonging to the Medicine PCP.

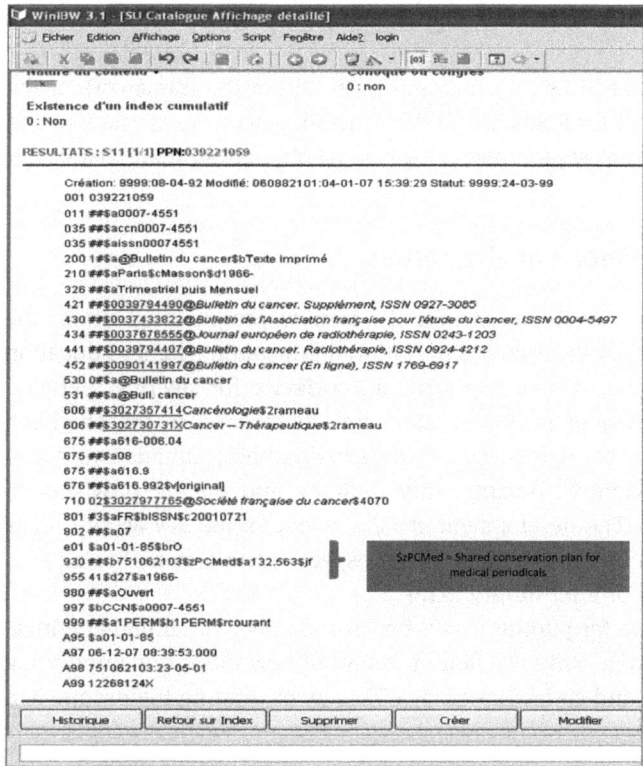

Figure 13.6

CTLes PCP co-facilitator

The definition of operational methods and communities of practice facilitates coordination and facilitation mechanisms. With the development since 2012 of the *Performing Arts PCP*, then in 2013 the *Philosophy PCP, Geography and Urban Planning*, and finally in 2014 the *Sports Science PCP*, CTLes has focused on making the system coherent and effective. The tools that have just been presented allow not just agents to perform numerous tasks but, above all, to act in an interactive and coherent way. Use of the *Collaborative Work Database* also allows each library to collect statistical data on transfers (volume of items sent and receipts as well as linear metres scrapped).

The dispersion of players within institutions in Ile-de-France and in the regions requires the use of transverse management of the different PCPs. This is done jointly by the CTLes and the library which carries the plan in its capacity as scientific referent.

Driving a Performance Logic

With the development of PCPs at a national level within the framework of the "*Collections of Excellence for Research (CollEx)*" arrangement, we are now seeing a paradigm shift, which now promotes a logic of results, rather than means.

The CollEx arrangement environment

Beginning in 2016, the development of PCPs is now programmed under the CollEx scheme initiated by the Ministry of National Education, Higher Education and Research. The CollEx system is a structuring device for steering, national coordination and pooling of resources that aims to respond to the changing documentary environment. It focuses on the development, enhancement and conservation of the scientific documentary heritage and on the provision of services for researchers. The development of PCPs is one of the key actions, as is the improvement of resources devoted to the retrospective conversion of catalogues and the modernisation of inter-library loans.

CTLes is responsible for piloting a call for projects open to all higher education and research libraries, with the aim of initiating new plans and supporting those already initiated and co-facilitated by CTLes by expanding their scope to a national level.

A total grant of €200 000 was allocated in 2016[5]. It will be distributed by CTLes to the establishments whose project has been selected and may cover part of the expenses related to the recruitment of temporary staff, logistics and the reporting and updating of collection status reports in SUDOC.

Successful projects may receive up to a maximum of 60% of the total amount envisaged. The maximum amount of the grant that could be allocated to a project is set at €50 000.

The selection committee, chaired by CTLes, has awarded a grant to the following projects co-facilitated by CTLes:

–   German, a new PCP co-facilitated by the National and University Library of Strasbourg;
–   Chemistry, a new PCP co-facilitated by the Joint Documentation Department of the University of Lyon 1;
–   Medicine, as part of the support for the conservation plan initiated in 2005 and co-facilitated by BIU Santé;
–   Physics, a new PCP co-facilitated by the Inter-Departmental Documentation Service of the University of Grenoble;

This process, within the framework of CollEx, which requires the compilation of a reasoned dossier presenting the scientific and pragmatic logic of each PCP, and its analysis by the selection committee, represents an evolution that will shake up the institutions.

Concrete implications

The main objective of a PCP is to offer researchers and teacher-researchers a body of sources precisely described in national tools (SUDOC) while guaranteeing an optimised service for accessing documents (PEB-FDD and/or unrestricted reader access).

For CTLes, it means supporting the libraries in their efforts to valorise the corpus, corresponding to the thematic segments concerned, through the specific tools it has developed, but also using know-how derived from experience gained over ten years.

From the outset, the presence of CTLes has proved necessary on the ground. It is the guarantee of quality training provided on a case-by-case basis to all participants for using tools as well as monitoring the different stages.

---

5 This grant will not be automatically renewable.

The launch of new shared conservation plans within the CollEx framework should strengthen the dynamics within the partner institutions around the tools developed by CTLes by streamlining the various stages in the *process* and limiting redundant operations. Indeed, among the participants in the new PCPs, some are already committed to ongoing plans.

The preferred approach is that of pragmatism and partner accountability. Without prejudging the difficulties inherent in implementing new plans, both in terms of defining the thematic perimeters and in terms of the tools' limits. It should be noted here that once the titles have been processed, the reference collections have been created and the catalogues updated, the activity continues until the institution decides to withdraw from the system.

The stages to follow

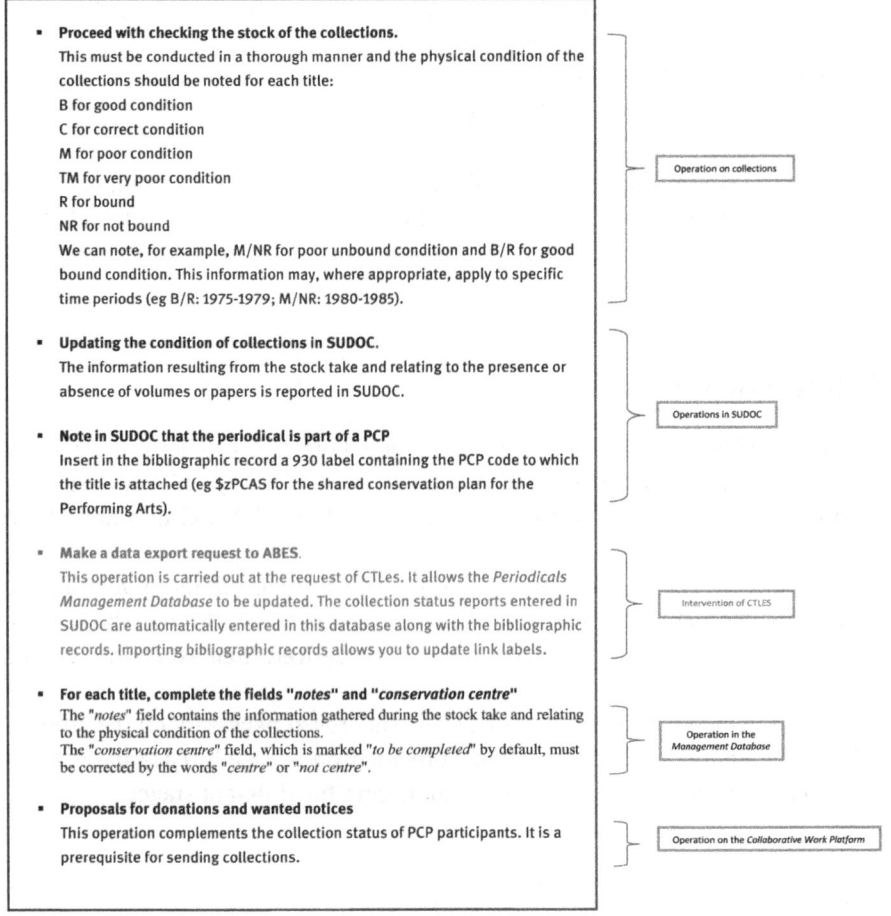

- **Proceed with checking the stock of the collections.**
  This must be conducted in a thorough manner and the physical condition of the collections should be noted for each title:
  B for good condition
  C for correct condition
  M for poor condition
  TM for very poor condition
  R for bound
  NR for not bound
  We can note, for example, M/NR for poor unbound condition and B/R for good bound condition. This information may, where appropriate, apply to specific time periods (eg B/R: 1975-1979; M/NR: 1980-1985).

  — Operation on collections

- **Updating the condition of collections in SUDOC.**
  The information resulting from the stock take and relating to the presence or absence of volumes or papers is reported in SUDOC.

- **Note in SUDOC that the periodical is part of a PCP**
  Insert in the bibliographic record a 930 label containing the PCP code to which the title is attached (eg $zPCAS for the shared conservation plan for the Performing Arts).

  Operations in SUDOC

- **Make a data export request to ABES.**
  This operation is carried out at the request of CTLes. It allows the *Periodicals Management Database* to be updated. The collection status reports entered in SUDOC are automatically entered in this database along with the bibliographic records. Importing bibliographic records allows you to update link labels.

  Intervention of CTLES

- **For each title, complete the fields "notes" and "conservation centre"**
  The "*notes*" field contains the information gathered during the stock take and relating to the physical condition of the collections.
  The "*conservation centre*" field, which is marked "*to be completed*" by default, must be corrected by the words "*centre*" or "*not centre*".

  Operation in the Management Database

- **Proposals for donations and wanted notices**
  This operation complements the collection status of PCP participants. It is a prerequisite for sending collections.

  Operation on the *Collaborative Work Platform*

Appropriate performance indicators

Indicators must be collected in the field by the teams that produce them, and are used to measure the activity and set the strategic directions of each plan.

1. Number of participants and their distribution across the national territory
2. Importance of the corpus by number of titles
3. Specifics of the corpus (only dedicated to the research level?)
4. Update level of the *Periodicals Management Database*
5. Number of transfers
6. Volume of collections transferred
7. Linear metres scrapped
8. Number of titles scrapped
9. Linear metres freed up in institutions

Santi Balagué i Linares and Lluís Anglada i de Ferrer

14 The GEPA, or how an old infantry barrack is an answer to the lack of space in Catalonia

1 Background

At the beginning of the 21st century, some Catalan university libraries detected a need stemming from the lack of space and the reconversion of physical libraries within the new European Higher Education panorama. With the same cooperative spirit that characterized former CBUC (Consortium of Academic Libraries of Catalonia, nowadays CSUC, Consortium of Academic Services of Catalonia) programs and services, the Consortium set in motion a project to address this need. An initial study was commissioned in 2002, and in 2003 a suitable building (old infantry barracks) was found in Lleida. The oficial opening took place in 2008.

The GEPA (Guaranteed Space for the Preservation of Access) facility is a cooperative repository, whose objectives are to store and preserve low use documents, ensuring their future access when needed, to convert room for books into room for library users, and doing it saving both space and money.

Main goals of this contribution are to comment the architectural project and its librarian issues, and to show how the GEPA facility allowed to change the spaces in university libraries in Catalonia. A brief historical introduction about the physical management of collections in llibràries is presented, and a short overview about high density library repositories all over the world, as an answer to the pressing problem of lack of spaces.

2 From off-campus to collective collections: historical panorama of library collections storage

Libraries, in order to guarantee the quality of their services, are in need of periodically reviewing their collections and transfering low-use books and documents from open access shelves to closed access stores. On occasions, the documents not selected for open access collections of the libraries often have a potential value for future users and must be conserved and accessible, and this need is

https://doi.org/10.1515/9783110535372-014

repeated in all libraries, which generates that unnecessarily duplicate documents are kept unnecessarily and that occupy multiple spaces that could have a more beneficial library use.

Libraries collect, order and keep books and other documents that are useful to their users. But not all library materials are used equally. Some, very used today, cease to be over time. Some documents that may have low use, do not have a low value. They represent the state of knowledge of mankind at a given moment. They have value for today's and tomorrow's students and they have to be conserved and well preserved. But they don't have to be preserved in the privileged spaces that are llibràries reading rooms. We can put them in stores and take this opportunity to reorganize the spaces according to the technological possibilities and the need of current libraries to offer social spaces and for the self-learning

Havig said so, there are many who think that collection management is not a fashion theme in the library community, and in relation to it, probably talking about shared high-capacity storage solutions must be one of the least trending topics nowadays. But on the other hand, it is becoming increasingly clear that the management of the library as an "infrastructure" must solve one of its great challenges, the traditionally and entropic expansive use of its spaces and its economic repercussion, it is worth to say.

It is said that the historical beginnings of remote warehouses may be found in the year 257 BC when the first universal research library in Alexandria began to "challenge its own storage capacity." Alexandria developed a plan for remote storage with a "library afillada" the Temple of Serapis, where at least 48,000 scrolls were kept, and grain warehouses at the port, where it is said that there were about 40,000 volumes. We do not know the space occupied by those parchments, but to respond to the growing lack of space for books and magazine volumes in the academic world, universities have been forced to seek creative solutions, often taking advantage of the growing spirit of Library collaboration

Collections management was a key issue in librarianship from the end of the 2nd World War and the mid-80s. Among many other things it was discovered that, on the one hand, the collections of research libraries tended to double the number of copies every sixteen years and, on the other, a significant number of cabbage documents The collection was very low. The growth of the collections has traditionally been faced with extensions of existing libraries or the construction of new buildings. But, since this can not always be done, the second solution has been to deposit potentially less-used documents in spaces with accessibility not so immediate as the open shelves of the library, that is, in stores.

The growth of the collection was pushing for documents with a real or potential low use to be stored in library stores or, sometimes, from outside the library. Obviously, the first qualitative leap was the storage of part of the 'off campus' library collection, but, once this was done, the established stores could be cooperative. These (such as the five that have the Ohio university system), work like a common deposit. Libraries share the costs of having an outside warehouse, but they do not manage the collection cooperatively.

The progressive digitization of information has only increased the volume of low-use information. Now it is not so much that the information is not used, but there are increasingly more digitized copies of magazines or books that were originally published in print, and in these cases, accessibility of the digital version makes it The printed original has a lower use than it had before. Thus, the old problem of storing traditional printed collections has not disappeared and continues to call for local and regional solutions.

In 2001, O'Connor study, Collier and Wells was one of the first cooperative approaches to the storage of library resources. At that time, the existence of different types of warehouses was checked: institutional, cooperative or collaborative (terms often used indistinctly but separated by the bibliography, understanding collaboration as a step beyond cooperation: spaces are shared, But also management costs and policies), regional and deposit libraries. The study reviewed some of the pioneering initiatives in Australia, Canada, the United States, Finland, France and the United Kingdom and gave a glimpse of the great issues of their management.

Later Lizanne Payne, then head of the Washington Research Library Consortium, reviewed the design of the storage facilities, the extent of their use and the context in which it occurred in the middle of the last decade. The study concluded that high-density storage equipment had become a key part of the university's library collection policy, and it was geared towards making the library community harness this collective capacity for Develop a broader perspective and promote a new approach in the management of collections that transcends institutional boundaries. In this regard, a recent study OCLC went a step further, proposing a "cloud-computing" libraries by combining these storage projects with the emergence of massive collections Of digitized documents.

3 What is the GEPA?

The GEPA equipment is a cooperative warehouse whose purpose is to preserve and preserve the documents of the libraries of the Libraries System of Catalonia with a low use, guarantee its future preservation and accessibility when required by a library. The objectives of the GEPA are to:

- Liberate library space and make it easier for them to reconvert part of the space currently devoted to saving books to create areas for study and learning.
- Be a download store for low or no use documents.
- Serve as a tool for a cooperative management of collections by the institutions that make up it.

The GEPA operates under a mixed hybrid model according to which a portion of documents are under a cooperative use regime and are managed cooperatively, and another part of the documents are under a regime of own use in which the institution that owns the documents is the one that establishes the rules of management and use of its documents. As regards to the documents for collaborative use, the number of copies that have been set previously will be kept according to the type of document. Once the GEPA has the maximum number of copies determined for a particular document, a copy kept in the GEPA can only be replaced by another one of a better quality.

The GEPA is a facility open to the public and can be used by all libraries of the Library System of Catalonia, anyone interested in the consultation of their collections and, in general, all the institutions that were accepted by the facility management commission. Access to the cooperative collection can be made in situ in the reading room, via electronic copies or photocopies, and via ILL. In addition, own use documents (which remain the property of each institution) can be used according to the norms established by the proprietary institution.

4 The GEPA facility planning

The Consortium of Academic Libraries of Catalonia (CBUC) was born in 1996 with the aim of creating and maintaining the union catalogue of the Catalan universities, *Catàleg Col·lectiu de les Universitats de Catalunya* (CCUC). A range of cooperative programmes has evolved, including interlibrary loan, consortial purchasing of electronic resources and a shared digital repository for theses. CBUC's aim was to improve library services through cooperation, and part of its history was to propose new cooperative programs. That was how it was considered to have a cooperative repository where storing low use print documents, so as to ensure its conservation and done with maximum efficiency So, in the tradition of the Consortium to propose new programs, the idea was to create a cooperative warehouse to store low-cost materials in such a way that their conservation was guaranteed and made with maximum efficiency.

The GEPA origins are found in the needs of the University of Barcelona (UB) library, for two reasons. First, the UB dimensions, it was one of the few Spanish ibraries that handled external storage for low use documents. UB Library director at that time, Ms Lamarca, is from the generation of librarians who were deeply impressed by the efficiency and effectiveness of the British Lending Division at Boston Spa (which later received the name of the British Library Document Supply Center), a generation that was capable to formulate a similar project in Spain, named National Loan Library, a project that, despite having buildings and staff, never saw the light.

CBUC's constants have always been to base its projects on international reality. In order to have a clear vision of what the project might consist of, in 2002, a study was commissioned to Joan Roca, Dean of Library Service from the Minnesota State University in Mankato. The report ("The collaborative storage option: a study by the Catalan libraries") on April 2003 and was later on examined and approved by the Technical Committee of the Consortium.

Joan Roca's study presented an historical summary of remote document storage systems. It also presents the results of a study conducted in 1999 by the Association of Research Libraries (ARL), the international association of research libraries, which is the most important source of information on these remote storage initiatives. The report deals with the physical features of librarian stores, the management issues related to the operation and services provided, and represents a snapshot of how ARL libraries used remote storage and high-lighted trends in its design, environmental conditions and services. Some results were that already in that year the majority of ARL libraries stored a large amount of material in remote buildings ("off-campus") and the pace of new construction or renovations of existing buildings to store had accelerated during the last decade. The new typical repository consisted on a cold storage building that made the most use of room through high density shelving.

CBUC libraries agreed to create a cooperative storage that received the name of GEPA which should help to preserve and store low-use documents. From a technical point of view it was agreed to admit two types of materials: own and collaborative documents, but to prioritise the collaborative collection, to which is devoted most of the space (80% of the facility). It was also decided that the collaborative collection does not duplicate items, unless it was required due to certain use circumstances.

Next undertaken step was the search for a possible location. Joan Roca's study showed that the best results for stores as the planned were obtained with new buildings, but it was also reported that the characteristics of these facilities made it possible to accept existing buildings. In our case, previously to the location of the site, the decision to use an existing building had been taken. With the help of the Catalan architect Josep Benedito, after considering various options the old infantry barracks of Gardeny Hill, in the city of Lleida, were chosen. Between 2004 and 2005, the rehabilitation project was completed and the financing of the rehabilitation works was agreed. The agreement for the creation of the GEPA involved the Lleida City Council, the CBUC, Catalan Ministers of Education and Culture, and the University of Lleida.

5 The GEPA transformation of military barracks to a library equipment

Historically, Gardeny hill in Lleida has enjoyed great strategic importance thanks to its situation and height above the rest of the nearby territory, which facilitated military operations and dominated much of the Ponent region, a plain area located in the westernmost part of Catalonia. Already in the Roman period it had been used with military objectives and centuries later the Order of the Temple was established, after which they had helped Ramon Berenguer IV to the recapture of the city of the Saracen domain. The result of this occupation was the result of a conventual set, which was extended and transformed into a new military fort in the 17th and 18th centuries. The current image of the monumental complex corresponds to the remains of what was an imposing fortress, while preserving numerous testimonies of the Templar sovereign site.

The last military activity that was hosted in the hill began during the 1940s with the construction of a set of military barracks. During the decade of 1985–95 the quarters were abandoned until, finally, in 1996 they were dismantled and sold in the Paeria de Lleida. At the moment, the artillery quartering is the headquarters of the Lleida Agri-Food Science and Technology Park, while the infantry quartering where the GEPA is located is being fitted with emblematic projects such as the Magical Media audiovisual production center.

5.1 Planning a compact storage facility

The objective of any project for compact storage must be to design an equipment that can save as many low-use documents as possible at the lowest cost. These documents must be kept in the best possible environmental conditions to extend their useful life. And all this, with the challenge of doing it in the most efficient way and giving the whole of the greatest functionality possible. Turning this aim is actually a complex task that should involve architects, engineers and librarians, and that it must ensure that the processes and services carried out are fast, safe, economical and sustainable.

Existing remotely storage experiences in some cases consist of a fairly close attachment and in others in a more distant building, the distances from the main campus vary from one to 150 kilometers. With respect to the design and location of these stores, there is a great variety of equipment, totally buried in tall buildings, of new constructions for the conversion of existing buildings or commercial buildings. Many are of modular design that makes it possible to add more units when needed.

Many of ongoing initiatives use the design features of the Harvard University Deposit System, the first high-density library store. These structures are usually large industrial buildings with high ceilings that allow high, adjustable, and open shelves. Bound volumes are stored in buckets, depending on their size, while the shelves have been designed based on the containers of the documents. Although this storage of materials according to size is the norm, there are some projects that opt for the usual classification libraries of the documentation for their subject.

As regards the distribution of spaces, it is essential to devote most of the material storage, but also to include areas to process them and to reserve queries for users. In some cases parts of the equipment are reserved to locate the special collections that require a specific security system. If we talk about the types of materials, storage sites often collect books and magazines with little circulation, but sometimes also files, special collections, films, photographs, and material on a microfit or magnetic format. One of the essential requirements for the success and acceptance of remote storage is that the inventory control and delivery systems are fast and effective. Most projects identify the materials stored in their catalog and link them to their exact location with barcodes or inventory control numbers. Some facilities use independent stock control systems but they can also manage the inventory through the same integrated library system.

Any experience of document storage must be considered control of environmental conditions. Over the last few years, there has been an evolution of the specifications of the design and consensus has emerged on its characteristics, the most remarkable that a constant control of the climate, with fresh and dry conditions, extend the life of the materials of the library collections. Existing projects emphasize the maintenance of constant conditions throughout the year. Light can also damage library's materials and well-conditioned venues have systems with low light and with limited lighting time of artificial light.

5.2 The GEPA renovation works

As it was said, GEPA is located in a military barrack that had been considered as a possible expansion of the University of Lleida. Most of the barracks became the embryo of today's technology park while some others were still available. It was easy to involve the University in the project and that the City Council saw this Catalan-scale equipment as an important asset and made it the transfer of one of the quarters that had not been assignat to the technology park. The location of the GEPA in one of the buildings of the barracks was agreed after a technical study determined that the building was adequate for the purpose.

Once the location was determined, works began to write the renovation draft of the barracks, which was based on indications from Joan Roca's foundational study. A public competition was held for the renovation project drafting and the technical management of the Gardeny building for GEPA. In February 2006 it was awarded to Albert Benet i Ferran, an architect from Lleida. Albert benet faced the challenge of combining the library needs with the exploitation of an existing building, a building that had good structural health, but due to years of neglect, it had problems regarding roofing, interior and exterior coatings, carpentry and installations. The project aimed to enable the maximum number of spaces for storage, along with support areas such as working areas, reading rooms, offices and some other required services and facilities.

The building has a H-shaped floor plan, which facilitates an ideal combination of the two -processing and storage- functions of the documents, because this plant allows the access to the central nucleus (the center bar of the H letter) services, work areas and distribution areas, while remaining in the two side wings (the two vertical bars of the H letter) free for deposits, with two modules of storage for each wing, and for on the three floors available to the building. The GEPA accesses are located on the ground floor of the central part, the main one for the front face (which leads to the main patio, ready for access and parking of vehicles, with a pergola that in case of weather conditions protects the download operations), like the secondary one in the back (that it gives to a patio landscaped). The main work room is located on the ground floor, while on the first floor there are offices, the consultation room, the meeting room and the scanning room, and on the second floor there is a multipurpose room that allows both work functions when processing needs increase, or meetings and other activities too. With regard to storage modules, these are communicated with the central block of the building, and each side block has a secondary staircase that communicates the modules between the different floors.

The rehabilitation project of the building was conceived and executed from budgetary restraint, making the most of the possibilities of the existing space, the collaboration between technicians and CBUC and the centralization of resources in favor of the role, of the documents. For this reason, much of the investment of the rehabilitation was used to isolate the building and thus favor the environmental conditions of preservation of the paper. Starting from a problem detected once the project started, related to the difficulty in fixing the plaster on the exterior walls of the facades, there was a twist on the project that improved its quality. Thus the team of the architect Benet decided to put the insulation out of the walls and fix the final plaster, which allowed to take advantage of the effect of thermal inertia of the structural walls as well as avoiding thermal bridges why the heat is dissipated. The thermal inertia achieved at the GEPA, with wide walls built by the military work in the 1940s, would allow the temperature stored during the summer to be used in winter and thus facilitate the maintenance of a constant temperature that prolongs the useful life of documents.

In the sense of environmental conditions for the preservation of paper, another consideration to be made is relative to light. The original building was full of windows on all facades, at a height above ground level much higher than usual, as surely it is proper in a military work as a defense system in the event of an attack. To protect the documents against the light, the solution posed by the technical team and agreed with the CBUC was to respect the exterior image of the facades (thus also maintaining the same aspect of the other quarters in the area and not breaking the homogeneity of the whole), but blinding all the windows from the inside in the storage modules.

The GEPA facility has a total built area of 5412 m2, of which over 3,700 m2 are used to store, in 12 storage modules. These storage modules have separate systems for the control of environmental conditions and are equipped with an automatic fire detection and suppression system, by water haze. When the maximum capacity is reached, it is expected to store, by compact shelving, about 43 kilometers from the current library open stacks. The building has two working areas to process the documents, one on the ground floor and one in the second floor, it has a reading room for twelve people, a document reproduction room, and a conference room.

6 Logistics and libraries

6.1 Compact shelving

When the concept of "compact" appears in the library world, the first thing that usually comes to mind is the mobile shelving rows, characterized by the maximization of the use of available surfaces. But between the usual organization of the documents in the consultation rooms, typically classified by subject, and the use of Compactus, there is a third way that is the compact storage, that pursues the efficiency in the use of spaces (or the volume, in a narrower sense) through the sorting of materials according to their sizes. Documents are stored in GEPA following the role model conceived in 1984 by Harvard University, the High Density Book Shelving System, also known as compact storage. Some system concepts to be considered are:

- Sorting of materials according to their size: Classify documents by their size and create different vertical shelving heights eliminates unused space in library stacks.
- The use of containers, in our case open cardbard trays or boxes, allows us to store at right angles, resulting in an increase in the density of the space used.
- Relation between physical space and information management. Coordination of shelves sizes with the containers used and and the documents in them, seeking maximum use of the shelf, both in terms of height and width.
- Use of lifting trucks. Access to aisles of shelves, with heights of more than ten meters is optimized (and ergonomically improved) with mechanical vehicles, called "picking" or lifting trucks.

6.2 Loads of documentation: from the reading rooms of the libraries to the modules of an industrial storage

As it has been said, the mixed model of operation of the GEPA includes a part of cooperative use and management documents, and another part of documents that are under a regime of own use. For this reason, the GEPA differentiates the loads of cooperative documentation (within the annual ordinary loads plans) of the loads carried out by the institutions with the materials that will become part of its own collection in the GEPA. It should also be taken into account that there may be documentation that is transported to the GEPA on a temporary basis, this may be when this documentation has (at least partially) the GEPA as a destination, for example, documents that are being processed in the GEPA to decide its final destination, or when this documentation temporarily occupies a space in the GEPA because, for example, renovation works are being done in the library of origin.

In this sense, one of the first studies carried out by the GEPA technical work group was the definition of the tasks that were to be executed to carry out the documentation loads, and then establish how each of them was to be performed. It was considered useful for its conceptualization to divide them into three types:

- Those related to the transport of the documentation, from their institutions of origin to facilities the GEPA
- Those of the technical treatment, more typical of the librarian world, such as the introduction of data to the system, in this case the Collective Catalog of the Universities of Catalonia.
- Those of the physical treatment (laborers), such as the cleaning of documents, their carving, assistance in technical treatment or final storage, for example.

To compensate for the inconvenience that "off-campus" storage can cause and pursuing the quality of any library service, the next step was to define the framework diagram of these tasks, to say where they had to be done by providing the greatest efficiency to the global set. Logistics pursue that any movement or storage that is carried out will be done giving the highest level of service at a reasonable cost. For this reason it is noteworthy to point out that from an initial scheme where most of the works were executed at the GEPA, they went to a redistribution where some of the tasks where made in the institutions of origin, so that greater efficiency to the whole process was achieved. Experiences such as the CARM Center of the CAVAL Australian consortium endorse this intermediate scheme of processes.

As for the execution of the tasks not assumed by the institutions of origin, both the transport and the technical processing and peonage, once the existence of enough companies with experience in the sector had been verified, it was decided to delegate the daily management through the outsourcing of services. Thus, the tasks of the GEPA are carried out by a company contracted by the Consortium under the direction of the facility manager and the relevant training of the company's personnel.

6.3 Libraries and logistics considerations

The relationship between buildings spaces and library management can also be at stake when it comes to considering the type of call number to be used for the location of the documents, although this connection may often be imperceptible. The identification of the documentation in the industrial storage rooms was a collaboration with logistics professionals, which lead to the creation of an ad hoc call number. To do this, a code was proposed that systematically identified each part of the building, from its most general to the detail of the boxes of each one of the shelves.

Another of the tasks that were carried out for the implementation of the GEPA was the creation of a conservation code. In order to optimize the operation of the service and the resources destined for interbibliotecary cooperation, the CBUC promoted the GEPA as a tool for cooperative collections management, which is why, within the cooperative collection, a maximum number of copies are established to be store for each title. Desirable, the selection of collections is made so that more copies of the established ones do not arrive at the equipment, but otherwise it is formulated to the proposed institutions for the elimination of transferred documents and which appear as duplicates. The choice of the documents to be loade is carried out regardless of the origin of the documents and prior assessment of the state of preservation of the items. To facilitate these tasks of comparing the status of the documents, either between copies stored in the GEPA versus the ones in the university libraries, or between the same items from diferent libràries, an alphanumeric code was created that reflects the state of preservation and quality of the documents. Three are the characteristics that are contemplated in the establishment of this code: the support (reflects the state of preservation of the paper), the type of binding, and the completeness of the collection.

7 From room for books to room for users in Catalan university libraries

Franco left a very poor library infrastructure that was necessary to supplement with measures taken after the 1983 University Reform law. As a result of the modernization of the Spanish university, the decade 1985 to 1995 was a very intense moment of organizational renewal, services creation and buildings contstruction for the Spanish university libraries. At the beginning of the 2000s, CBUC libraries clearly saw two things that influenced in the creation of GEPA: it would not be easy to get money to expand the libraries that had been recently created no more than ten years ago, and that they began to be saturated due to the accumulated documents, and that the digitization of journals was an unstoppable movement that would reduce the need for physical items available to users.

However, there was a third factor which had great influence in the creation of the store: the desire to transform library spaces so as these spaces could accommodate group work activities with special equipments. In 2002, REBIUN (the Spanish association of university libraries) adopted a strategic plan that represented an organizational change to the association and the establishment of new priorities. The first strategic issue wanted to promote "the construction of a new model of university library, conceived as an essential and active part of a system resources for the learning and research." This new approach prompted a profound transformation of libraries into CRAI (Learning and Research Resource Centres) CRAI main feature is to integrate in the library audiovisual, technology and librarian services and resources, which requires changing the interior design of libraries. Before libraries were designed to use books, and nowadays they are designed so that people can interact among them with all the resources and services the library has.

This new orientation of libraries could not be translated into new buildings, as they had been recently built. To do so, there was no other alternative but to transform the existing spaces. GEPA is an assistant in the task of transforming library spaces, because it allows low-use documents to be kept in its store rooms, freeing space formerly dedicated to books and allowing people to occupy them. Below there are some examples of how GEPA facility allowed to change the spaces in university libraries in Catalonia. Here there rar some examples of physical changes in Catalan libraries after large loads of documents to GEPA.

Adaptation to EEES, Universitat Autònoma de Barcelona, 2009–2010

In 2009, Universitat Autònoma de Barcelona (UAB), in their efforts for the architectural adaptation to the needs of the Bologna Process, executed some works in their libraries. They needed the collaboration of GEPA to front the emergency storage needs of the Library of Science and Technology, the Sabadell University Library and the University Library of Medicine (Sant Pau Hospital). As a result of this action, for example, they created a users learning room at BCT

University campus remodeling, Universitat Politècnica de Catalunya, 2010

The Universitat Politècnica de Catalunya (UPC) is the largest engineering university in Catalonia. With more than 25 schools, it is located in several cities, as Barcelona, Castelldefels or Terrassa. North Campus, located in Barcelona, is one of UPC main campus, in 2010 UPC began renovation works in many of the buildings, amongst them the library (Biblioteca Rector Gabriel Ferraté, BRGF). GEPA and UPC worked together with loads of materials from the library.

From libraries to CRAI: Universitat Rovira i Virgili, 2013

In 2013 there was a close relationship between libraries of Universitat Rovira i Virgili (URV) and GEPA. On the one hand, the Library of the Faculty of Medicine and Health Sciences undertook a renovation of spaces for their adaptation to URV CRAI. Also, in CRAI Campus Bellissens urgent action needed to make a transfer of low-use documents from their deposit. And in CRAI Campus Sescelades had the collaboration of GEPA to load documents to remodel some of its spaces.

8 The GEPA advantages and its improvement possibilities

The reason for CBUC's projects is to respond to the needs of its consortium. In the case of the GEPA, once the needs of the Catalan university libraries were detected in the early 2000s, the CBUC opted for a benchmarking process, embracing the original solutions already raised in the United States. A base study was promoted, and the experience and knowledge of architects was needed for the location of the spaces and the drafting of the basic lines of the rehabilitation project and for the final concretion of the architectural design. This is one of the most gratifying evaluations of this route, by sharing the views from the different professional areas when it comes to responding to the needs that the project raised, be it in its origin, as then with the realities and setbacks found in any construction or rehabilitation work. From a librarian point of view, contact with professionals in architecture and engineering helped to base some of our starting points and facilitated the approach to decision areas that are less common to us.

Although most of the high-density storage projects in the world are committed to the construction of new buildings, the GEPA proves that the use of an existing building is possible and has its advantages. The maximum to keep documents at the lowest possible cost is facilitated by a content rehabilitation project when the characteristics of the original building correspond to the needs to be satisfied. That is why the preliminary study that defined librarians' questions was correct, and the later putting them in common with the architects who had to put it into practice. One of the possibilities of improvement would be to include in this game of detection of needs and design of solutions the participation of logistics professionals, that could analyze the best options for the circuits of the goods and the transport of these, besides opening the range of possibilities to the sector.

The GEPA achieved the involvement of the stakeholders in the project, among other reasons, thanks to the application of a technically unquestionable logic response to the library needs detected. The equipment saves space storing documents compactly and makes it possible, by working together, to free spaces in the campus and city centers and create the inertias with which to reduce the unnecessary costs of saving more books than necessary. The GEPA was developed thanks to a vision shared by public institutions, it was the result of joint work among specialists from different fields and is made great through the cooperation between libraries.

9 References

Anglada i de Ferrer, Lluís and Margarita Taladriz Mas. 1997. « Pasado, presente y futuro de las bibliotecas universitarias espanÞolas. » Arbor 157:617–618.

Cabo, Mercè, Sonsoles Celestino, Carmen Guerra and Margarita Taladriz Mas. 2003. "Un puente hacia el futuro: El Plan Estratégico de REBIUN." BiD: Textos Universitaris De Biblioteconomia i Documentació 10. http://bid.ub.edu/10cabo2.htm.

Dempsey, Lorcan. 2006. "Libraries and the Long Tail: Some Thoughts about Libraries in a Network Age." D-Lib Magazine 12(4). http://www.dlib.org/dlib/april06/dempsey/04dempsey.html.

Dempsey, Lorcan. 2012. "Thirteen Ways of Looking at Libraries, Discovery, and the Catalog Scale, Workflow, Attention." Educause Review. http://www.educause.edu/ero/article/thirteen-ways-looking-libraries-discovery-and-catalog-scale-workflow-attention.

Dempsey, Lorcan, Brian F. Lavoie, Constance Malpas, Lynn Silipigni Connaway, Roger C. Schonfeld, J.D. Shipengrover, and Günter Waibel. 2013. Understanding the Collective Collection: Towards a System-wide Perspective on Library Print Collections. Dublin, Ohio: OCLC Research. http://www.oclc.org/content/dam/research/publications/library/2013/2013-09.pdf.

Domínguez Aroca, Isabel. 2005. "La biblioteca universitaria ante el nuevo modelo de aprendizaje: docentes y bibliotecarios, aprendamos juntos porque trabajamos juntos." RED : Revista De Educación a Distancia 4: 1–25. http://www.redalyc.org/articulo.oa?id=54709706.

Malpas, Constance. 2011. Cloud-sourcing Research Collections: Managing Print in the Mass-digitized Library Environment. Dublin, Ohio: OCLC Research. http://www.oclc.org/research/publications/library/2011/2011-01.pdf.

Malpas, Constance and Brian F. Lavoie. 2014. Right-scaling Stewardship: A Multi-scale Perspective on Cooperative Print Management. Dublin, Ohio: OCLC Research. http://www.oclc.org/research/publications/library/2014/oclcresearch-cooperative-printmanagment-2014.html.

Manguel, Alberto. 1996. A History of Reading. New York: Viking.

O'Connor, Steve, Andrew Wells and Mel Collier. 2002. "A Study of Collaborative Storage of Library Resources." Library Hi Tech 20(3): 258–269.

Payne, Lizanne. 2007. Library Storage Facilities and the Future of Print Collections in North America. Dublin, Ohio: OCLC Programs and Research. http://www.oclc.org/programs/publications/reports/2007-01.pdf.

Rider, Fremont. 1944. The scholar and the Future of the Research Library: A Problem and its Solution. New York: Hadham Press.

Roca, Joan. 2003. L'opció de magatzem col·laboratiu: Un estudi per a les biblioteques catalanes. Barcelona: CBUC.

Saarti, Jarmo and Pentti Vattulainen. 2013. "Management of and Access to Print Collections in National and Repository Libraries in Europe: Collection for Use or for Preservation." Library Management 34(4/5): 273–280.

Bernard F. Reilly, Jr.

15 Sharing Print Serials in North America: A Status Report and Agenda for the Next Decade

The evidence is mounting that the integrity of the vast, encyclopedic print collections built and long maintained by North American libraries is now in jeopardy. The corpus of print journals, newspapers, books, and other paper-based materials, many published on acidic and highly unstable paper, is aging, and physical fragility and inherent vice loom as ever larger threats. More-over, pressure on libraries to reduce print holdings and reallocate space to other uses is intense and growing, increasing the likelihood that important materials will be lost in the process. The center of gravity in U.S. and Cana-dian research and academic libraries is shifting from collections to digital resources, and collection management is giving way to other library roles and responsibilities.

In response to these conditions recent years have seen the rise of co-operative print archiving and sharing initiatives by academic libraries in North America: Scholars Trust, an effort of the Association of Southeast Research Libraries (ASERL); the Western Regional Storage Trust (WEST) based the Western U.S., and COPPUL SPAN, a project of the Consortium of Prairie and Pacific Uni-versity Libraries in Canada, to name just a few. Those initiatives brought new practices, systems, and tools to bear on the evolving struggle to deal with a chronic and worsening shortage of collections space on library campuses.

Limitations of the Status Quo

Unfortunately, despite the investment of considerable time and resources, only a small fraction of the existing serial literature in North American libraries is encompassed by the programs. A CRL analysis of the major U.S. and Canadian shared print serial programs found a number of limitations. At a June 2015 summit of the major U.S. and Canadian print archive and shared print programs, sponsored by The Andrew W. Mellon Foundation, CRL presented an analysis of the collective serial archiving efforts to date, using data on retained journals aggregated in the PAPR database (http://papr.crl.edu/). The analysis revealed major limitations in the scope and quality of the archiving activity.

https://doi.org/10.1515/9783110535372-015

Specifically, as of June 2015:

a. *Only a small portion of the universe of published serials was covered by the existing archiving and shared print programs.* Measured in terms of the percentage of serial titles published in the past 100 years, the number of serial titles archived by credible programs was small. While millions of volumes were being archived by established print archiving and sharing programs, the percentage of existing titles actually archived in a meaningful way were estimated to be no more than two percent.

b. *Redundancy among the archives of print serials was minimal and sporadic.* Of the 71,527 unique titles registered in PAPR, only 13,513 (19%) appeared to be held by more than one archiving program. In general, the amount of duplication across all archives was minimal and, ironically, was concentrated on materials that were also available in electronic form.

c. *Humanities and Social Science titles were only sparsely archived.* Titles in LC class Q (Science) made up 25% of the titles archived; followed by Technology (T) at 22% and Social Science (H) a distant third at 9%.

d. *Most shared print and print archiving efforts focused on secondary, rather than primary, literature.* Not surprisingly, scholarly and scientific journals dominated the holdings of most print archive and shared print programs, while trade journals, popular serials, and industrial literature were archived by relatively few programs.

e. *Historical materials were not well covered.* A disproportionate number of the serial titles archived, as a percentage of the total number of serials published in a given year, date from the late twentieth century.

f. *The overwhelming majority of titles archived were in English.* English-language serials represented 78% of the titles archived in programs registered in PAPR.

The analysis also suggested that the archiving programs to date provided a relatively weak safety net:

a. *Precise information about archived holdings was scarce.* The information available about the terms of archiving and shared print programs fell short of the granularity and detail needed to support sound risk assessments and decision-making on preserving, retaining, and disposition of serial materials.

b. *Actionable information about archive programs was scarce.* Information about the commitments made by archiving libraries to verify and maintain archived runs of serials, and information about the measures in place to fulfill those archiving obligations, was often unavailable or lacked sufficient detail to inform the decisions of stakeholder libraries.

c. *Volume was more common than value as a criterion for selecting materials for archiving.* Because recovering space occupied by print journals is an imperative for many libraries most programs were designed to achieve coverage of the largest amount of material, in terms of space reclaimed and number of volumes archived.

d.   *Most programs archived materials "in place", as opposed to extracting and isolating archived materials in dedicated environments.* Reliance upon extant runs of titles currently in campus stacks or remote storage, rather than assembling and isolating holdings for the purpose of archiving, was a common practice. This was the least expensive and least disruptive approach to creating designated archives of titles.

e.   *The programs varied considerably in the benefits and incentives they provide.* The benefits archiving programs provide to participating libraries differ from one program to another. A variety of incentives for participation existed, some weaker and shorter-lived than others.[1]

The CRL data suggested that the scale and scope of print archiving would have to be dramatically increased to prevent the loss of the important print serial literature collected and preserved by U.S. and Canadian research libraries. Strategies adopted by the cooperative print archiving/sharing efforts needed to be better aligned, to ensure that the most important and endangered materials are identified and preserved. In short, what was needed was a blueprint for a systematic approach to preserving an important component of the North American "knowledge base."

In April 2018, CRL convened *@Risk: Stewardship, Due Diligence and the Future of Print*, a public forum attended by representatives of over 120 U.S. and Canadian universities, colleges and independent research libraries, publishers, and preservation organizations. Attendees explored the meaning of due diligence and responsible stewardship in this particularly fraught environment. Discussions, and presentations by thought leaders in the field, were to provide the basis for blueprinting a North American cooperative agenda on collections and preservation.

The forum discussions and subsequent conversations with individuals at libraries, universities, and funding agencies suggested that focused, decisive action was needed to ensure that the rich and unique legacy of centuries of library investment would endure. The American shared print programs, it was decided, would have to allocate new resources in a sustained effort at scale to shift the burden of preserving the "critical corpus" of published serial literature from individual libraries to the collective.[2]

---

1 The agenda, analysis and final report of the PAPR II summit are online at: http://www.crl. edu/node/11334.

2 The agenda and presentations from the @Risk forum are available at www.crl.edu/node/ 11919.

Over the previous ten years CRL had made a meaningful start in that direction. In 2012 CRL and the Linda Hall Library of Science, Engineering and Technology (LHL), an independent research Library based in Kansas City, Missouri, formed a strategic partnership. The purpose of the partnership was to preserve, further develop and provide access to historical research collections in the fields of science, technology, and engineering, exploiting the rich holdings of print serials in those fields assembled by the two institutions during the past six decades.

The combined CRL and LHL serial holdings constitute a premier library of global science and technology serials, consisting of more than 90,000 titles including:
- Current and back file STE print serials from Elsevier, Wiley, Springer, and other publishers
- Historical serials published by the Russian Academy of Sciences and other learned societies in Europe, Asia, and the U.S.
- Foreign serials in the fields of Physics, Chemistry, and Engineering received through the Library of Congress Cooperative Acquisition Program

The partnership entailed a radical approach to collection sharing. Serial holdings of both institutions would be digitized to preservation standards and, under certain specified conditions, merged. In planning the new arrangement CRL established ground rules for handling other appropriate CRL collections in the same way. As CRL collections become more fragile and difficult to replace, it was clear that cooperative digitization arrangements were likely to become more important. The process of creating the partnership created a template for the merging of print archiving and cooperative digitization.

The partnership had important safeguards. The "right of first refusal" granted CRL by LHL formalized CRL's claim to any merged volumes in the unlikely event that LHL were to disperse its collection assets. In such an event LHL collections, being extremely valuable, would likely be placed with a worthy successor organization, perhaps a CRL affiliate with a similar collecting focus. By terms of the agreement CRL would also be in possession of high-quality digital files of all issues of the journals.

A New Shared Collections Agenda for 2017–2026

Over the course of its history CRL had assembled the largest shared collection of print materials in North America, preserving and maintaining them in a purpose-built collections facility, and making them available through ILL and document delivery. In recent years digitization and partnerships enabled CRL to improve access to a corpus of nearly 50,000 serials, while safeguarding those materials for the long term. In 2016 it became apparent that even those efforts would no longer scale to the challenges North American libraries were then facing. CRL analysis, and the conversations at the @*Risk Forum*, indicated that the pressure on libraries to divest of print was intensifying, and that the size of the corpus of humanities and social science print serials worthy of preservation in U.S. academic libraries was enormous, upwards of 500,000 titles.

As a blueprint for that effort In December 2016 CRL promulgated an agenda for expanding the North American shared collections over the next decade. The agenda consisted of five elements:

1) Substantially expanding the scope and improving the quality of the shared collections.
2) Merging preservation and electronic access.
3) Creating and promoting consensus on the scope, norms and standards of print stewardship.
4) Forging and formalizing new partnerships to achieve greater scale.
5) Articulating and promoting a clear and convincing narrative for scholars and funders.

The agenda was designed to enable, over the next ten years, the costs of maintaining the corpus to be radically reduced and redistributed, while generating new benefits for North American scholars and libraries.

Expanding the Scope and Improving the Quality of the Shared Collections

CRL and the Linda Hall Library currently provide access to a combined 90,000 serial titles from their collections. Most North American shared print programs focus on widely held materials, i.e., English-language publications in the STEM fields published in the 1970s and later. Therefore shared print programs should prioritize earlier serials that are relevant to humanities and social science (HSS) research.

Moreover, efforts should invest in print sharing activities that combine preservation and strategic collection development, identifying and assembling secure and well-curated serial collections and working to improve their quality, integrity and comprehensiveness. This will entail actively identifying materials of interest, gathering and analyzing detailed data about archived serial holdings and repositories, filling gaps in the archived serial holdings, and other measures to ensure the long-term integrity and completeness of the shared collections.

Merging Preservation and Electronic Access

Because the benefits of archiving are multiplied when accompanied by services like digital access and interlibrary loan, libraries should substantially increase investment in digitizing serials both on a systematic basis and in response to researcher requests. It is necessary to significantly increase the number of important serial titles that are both adequately preserved and digitally accessible to North American libraries. The CRL and the Linda Hall partnership provides liberal interlibrary loan, and rapid electronic delivery of approximately 12,000 articles, another 478,000 pages digitized on request for researchers, and another 8,000 or so volumes digitized each year on a systematic basis. Most shared print programs, however, provide only limited interlibrary loan and article delivery. It was clear that to justify sustaining, let alone expanding investment in, the archiving efforts the programs would have to deliver more value to scholars, namely fast and convenient delivery on a 24/7 basis.

That task is complicated by copyright restrictions on digitization and web distribution of materials produced in the twentieth-century or later. However, those restrictions will have to be overcome for print sharing to remain viable.

Consensus on the Scope, Norms and Standards of Print Stewardship

Sustainability requires clear and realistic strategic goals. The immense pool of knowledge, experience and expertise of the librarians and scholars in the U.S. and Canadian academic libraries community can provide an intellectually defensible basis for decisions on the appropriate level of redundancy, service, transparency, and care of the shared collections. However, the new norms and standards for stewardship should be rigorous.

Historically CRL has set a high bar for stewardship: a supporting organization incorporated as an entity with full legal standing; governed by formal bylaws and an elected board accountable to the stakeholders; and capable of owning property and entering into contracts that are legally binding. The respective commitments to print of CRL and the Linda Hall Library rest upon the foundation of a dedicated, bricks-and-mortar collections facility, sound and audited financial practices, and combined assets of over $200 million. Moreover, the cooperative agreement governing the partnership is executed at the chief executive level between two legal entities, i.e., a non-profit corporation (CRL) and a trust (LHL), and therefore has legal enforceability. The LHL collections are central to the institution's mission; do not circulate; and are maintained in a secure, climate-controlled physical environment.

Finally, funding is guaranteed to Linda Hall by CRL in return for explicitly defined services. The services include document delivery of articles from over 3,500 current STE serial titles and 40,000 retrospective STE titles through RapidILL, and digitization of historical serials to preservation standards. Linda Hall will continue to develop its serial collections, governed by a joint collection development policy adopted by CRL and LHL in 2015.

Such features are essential to the ability of stakeholder libraries to guarantee researchers long-term access to shared resources, while avoiding the costs of creating and maintaining those resources locally. Today the terms of steward-ship are critical to the same libraries' ability to manage down print responsibly, to make decisions that are consequential, and in some cases irreversible.

Forging and Formalizing New Partnerships to Achieve Greater Scale

To achieve the scale necessary to adequately preserve the serial print corpus, North American shared print programs will need to work together to achieve a rational and sustainable division of labor that avoids unnecessary and costly duplication of efforts. CRL's efforts for the next decade will focus on the critical corpus of over 500,000 serials that support humanities and social science research.

Identifying the appropriate and capable partners and setting adequate terms for shared services is the next step. The ideal profile of candidate organizations is becoming apparent. Major U.S. and Canadian research libraries and "libraries of record", with deep and extensive HSS holdings, and that have longstanding commitments to comprehensive collecting, are the natural candidates to form the core of such a network. Libraries and cooperative shared print programs that can provide the requisite commitments both to archive and provide elec-tronic access to serial holdings will be well positioned to play a role in the new network.

Future investment in shared print will have to be both strategic and equitable. Most libraries involved in U.S. and Canadian shared print programs are also CRL members. They currently bear the lion's share of the cost of the North American shared print efforts, and the cost of other public goods supported by CRL. The calculus on forming the new network will then have to take those libraries' investment into account, to avoid wasteful and unfair duplication or redun-dancy of effort. An equitable exchange of services and benefits among the North American shared print programs and libraries of record must be devised. This will take some careful thinking as we move forward.

As the network takes shape, participating libraries must also determine how many distributed copies of a given serial are enough, how strong the commitments on archiving should be, to what extent archiving commitments should be audited, and what services archiving partners must provide. All of those services will have a cost, and so agreements must be structured to ensure a return to participating libraries that matches their investment.

A Clear and Convincing Narrative

Despite formidable new budgetary constraints, librarians remain answerable to scholars for whom access to the physical artifact continues to be indispensable. Therefore the supporting narrative of North American print sharing must emphasize the "new goods" that the preservation efforts create, to counter the perception that managing down library collections necessarily entails the loss or degradation of scholarly assets. Once again, then, providing electronic access to archived print materials will be critical to the success of the new effort.

CRL's Evolving Role

During the past decade CRL began to evolve from an organization that primarily built and maintained shared collections to one that ensures long-term access to shared resources. Since then the continued migration of knowledge and information to the digital realm has combined with a measurable deterioration in the supply chain for tangible (print and microform) materials, to challenge the organization's ability to continue to support advanced research. These developments require that CRL now accelerate its transformation and bring its operations to greater scale.

There will be new financial challenges, and so aligning vision with resources will be critical to success. Throughout its history CRL has been, among other things, a mechanism for such alignment. In keeping with that history CRL must now help achieve a new consensus among the other players on priorities, standards and services, with libraries deciding what they can and will support.

Given the state of public finances in the U.S. and Canada at the federal and state or provincial levels, it is not likely that much additional funding will become available for shared print in the U.S. and Canada. Aspirations will therefore have to be scaled to the level of resources the libraries can currently provide, and a larger population of North American libraries will have to be persuaded to invest. Every new partnership and initiative must be judged on the basis of its ability to generate tangible new benefits for libraries.

Guided by a Board of Directors and Collections and Services Policy Committee representing over 200 U.S. and Canadian libraries, CRL is now engaged in forging community consensus on what is both desirable and affordable. Its shared collection agenda is actually the product of years of discussion and deliberation by representatives of member universities – public and private – and four-year colleges, from all regions of the U.S. and Canada.

In 2017 CRL began to narrow its focus to grow and preserve collections essential to its core mission, and to reallocate resources to this effort from preserving materials of little and diminishing value to its members. With time this will permit a shift in the balance between CRL fixed assets (bricks and mortar, centralized collections) and liquid assets that are more conducive to expanding the shared collections and the services built around those collections.

It is important to note that even with these reallocations CRL's total annual investment in collections and collection-related resources – its core value – will still be greater than it was five years ago. CRL's commitment to the integrity and accessibility of critical documentation and evidence remains undiminished, but its ability to fulfill its mission will be strengthened. The end is the same but the means are different.

In moving forward there will no doubt be losses. North American libraries individually have always had to choose between collecting and maintaining materials that will survive elsewhere in one form or another, and those that will surely disappear absent their intervention. It is now time to bring that capability to bear on consequential action at a much greater scale.

About the authors

Santi Balagué i Linares
Consorci de Serveis Universitaris de Catalunya,
GEPA Facility manager

Jean-Louis Baraggioli
Centre technique du livre de l'enseignement
supérieur Paris

Alasdair Ball
The British Library

Jonny Edvardsen
National Library of Norway

Lluís Anglada i de Ferrer
Consorci de Serveis Universitaris de Catalunya
(CSUC), Barcelona

Linda George
University of Auckland

Brigitte Kromp
Vienna University Library

Wolfgang Mayer
Vienna University Library

Ulrich Niederer
Zentral- und Hochschulbibliothek Luzern

Steve O'Connor
Director and Principal, Information
Exponentials Pty Ltd

Christian Oesterheld
Zentralbibliothek Zürich

Bernie Reilly
Center for Research Libraries, Chicago

Helen Renwick
University of Auckland

Michael Robinson
Chief Executive Officer, CAVAL Ltd.

Jarmo Saarti
Library Director, University of Eastern Finland

Helen Sakrihei
The National Library of Norway

Peter Sidorko
University Librarian, University of Hong Kong

Pentti Vattulainen
National Repository Library of Finland

Liz White
The British Library

About the editors

Pentti Vattulainen

Pentti Vattulainen (FL K 1) is a Finnish librarian who has long worked in the National Repository Library (NRL) of Finland. From the beginning Pentti has contributed to its development to be a leading international model of a functioning repository as a shared national storage facility and interlibrary lending centre. He has recently been made a Knight, 1 class, of the Order of the Lion of Finland.

Pentti has written dozens of articles on interlibrary lending and resource sharing as well as on collection management, collection policy and library co-operation in Finnish, Nordic and international journals. He has been member of the editorial board of many journals including Library Management. He made a study on **Performance of Interlending in Nordic Academic Libraries**, 2003. He was the chief editor of the fifth edition of **Handbook on the international Exchange of Publications**, De Gruyter Saur 2005.

He has been active in IFLA chairing two committees: Acquisition and Collection Development (2007–2011) and Document Delivery and Resource Sharing (2013–2017). He has been a speaker or organiser in several national, Nordic, European and international events including IFLA International Interlending Conferences. He has a conference series of his own: **Kuopio**. This conference series has concentrated on issues connected with keeping print library materials available in the fast-changing library environment. **Kuopio 6** conference will be held in Basel, Switzerland on 14–16 March 2018, where this new book will be published.

Steve O'Connor

Steve is a seasoned international speaker, workshop presenter, editor, author, consultant and, of course, librarian. He wrote the book on scenario planning for libraries and other information organizations (*Imagining Your Library's Future* Chandos which is now also being published in the Chinese language by the National Library of China). His next book was titled *Library Management in disruptive times* (published by Facet) while this new title is: *Repositories for Print: strategies for Access, Preservation and Democracy* De Gruyter, 2018.

He is a long standing journal editor (*Library Management and Collection and Curation*), the author of over 70 articles as well as a frequent presenter at international conferences and also a Workshop Presenter. He has presented at many universities. Most recently, he has been working on a Masters for Information Leadership at Charles Sturt University where he is an Adjunct Professor. Steve's passion is to foster creative and dynamic imaginative communities that deliver positive and measureable results for their Library's customers. Understanding that there are many paths to the Future is allowing us to pause, reflect and to really think differently rather than have our Futures determined for us.

http://www.informationexponentials.com/home/

Index

Compiled by Laurence Storey